home, paper, scissors

Decorative Paper Accessories for the Home

Patricia Zapata

POTTER
CRAFT
New York

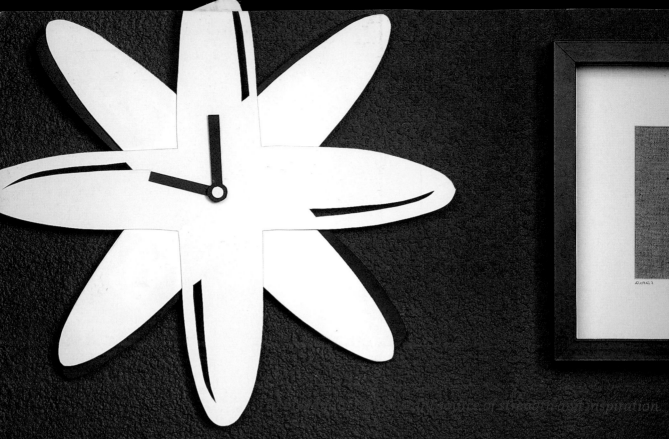

Published in the United States by Potter Craft, an imprint of the
Crown Publishing Group, a division of Random House, Inc., New York.

www.crownpublishing.com

wwww.pottercraft.com

POTTER CRAFT and colophon is a registered trademark of Random House, Inc.

Library of Congress Cataloging-in-Publication Data
Zapata, Patricia.
   Home, paper, scissors : decorative paper accessories for the home /
Patricia Zapata. — 1st ed.
      p.   cm.
   Includes index.
   ISBN 978-0-307-45282-5
   1. Paper work.   2. Interior decoration accessories.   I. Title.
   TT870.Z32   2009
   745.54—dc22   2008044046

Printed in China

Design by Chi Ling Moy
Photography by Sanford Schulwolf

How-to photography by Patricia Zapata
Styling by Patricia Zapata
Technical editing by Kevin Kosbab

10   9   8   7   6   5   4   3   2   1

First Edition

CONTENTS

PREFACE

I have always loved paper. Like many small children, I started doodling and drawing at a young age. There was never a shortage of paper around the house. We used it to create our masterpieces, or we'd send it soaring through the air in the shape of airplanes. When I started school, there was nothing better than to hold a brand-new notebook in my hands. That first blank page was always so welcoming. I don't recall when it happened, but I eventually began collecting paper—all different colors and textures. It became increasingly difficult even to consider writing on any of these treasures.

Things haven't changed much. Today I have more paper in the house than I know what to do with. The unwanted paper we get in our mailbox, junk mail, gets used on occasion for some project or other. I even save the security envelopes that have interesting patterns printed inside. Because I am a graphic designer, paper samples flood my office, too, giving me a glimpse of the latest in the paper industry. And don't even get me started about how tempted I feel to walk out of a craft store with an armful of yet more paper-related items! Like I said, I love paper. I also love to find new and unexpected uses for it, and I enjoy sharing these paper projects with others.

Which brings us to this book. I don't know how many times I've heard people say, "I could never make something like that." My standard reply is, "That isn't true." I truly believe that with the right tools, a bit of time, and an inspiring project, anyone can turn a simple sheet of paper into something interesting and useful. That is what this book is about. It's about giving you the inspiration and know-how to dive in with a pair of scissors and create something that you may not have tried otherwise. The satisfaction of a completed project will be your reward. Using a project to enhance your home, incorporating it on a dinner table, or offering it as a gift to others will be an added bonus.

The projects in this book don't require any previous experience with papercrafts, and they won't take up much of your time. Best of all, they're not very expensive to make. I specifically designed all the projects so that they can be customized by adding embellishments or simply changing the color of the paper used to match your taste and decor.

In my crafts, I'm very inspired by nature and paper's humble, organic origins. As you work with paper, you'll no doubt find your own personal style and inspiration as well. For those of you who are trying to be more eco-friendly papercrafters, there are several projects—like the Magazine Bowl (page 96)—that reuse items you probably already have in your home.

I hope the projects in this book will offer you a worthwhile experience with this material and enough inspiration to further develop your own ideas. More importantly, I hope you have fun!

Patricia Zapata

The Basics of Papercraft

There has never been a better time to enter the world of papercraft. The sheer amount of paper available today allows for all tastes and needs to be represented. The tools that are used in this medium also vary from a simple pair of scissors to more advanced cutter templates. But for me, one of the exciting aspects of papercraft is that most any idea can be made with the simplest of tools and paper that can be found in your nearest craft supply store. In this book I keep the materials and tools needed for each project accessible and easily adaptable to suit your unique skill set and personal taste. Explore the many possibilities that spring into your mind as you discover materials that are new to you.

PAPER

There is such a variety of paper available that it's helpful to narrow your choices by deciding the look and feel you'd like your project to have. Do you want it to appear more organic? Work with handmade and textured papers. Do you want your project to seem more contemporary? Work with matte or glossy smooth finishes. If you'd like to be more conscientious about the materials you use, recycled paper is also something to consider. If you'd like to save time, premade paper embellishments can be added to give a project more personality.

Paper is divided into two main categories: size and weight. Sizes are standardized in Europe by the ISO system (which uses A2, A4, and A6) and in North America by the classifications of letter, legal, and tabloid. For the purposes of this book, and to simplify our efforts, inches (") and millimeters (mm) or centimeters (cm) are provided for all projects.

Weight is given in pounds (lb). The weight or thickness of a sheet is very important for the success of a project. In this book I've further divided the weight of paper into three main categories:

Lightweight (10–30 lb): This group includes kraft paper, tissue paper, origami paper, newsprint, office paper, stationery, and some handmade papers.

Medium weight (60–80 lb): This group includes some handmade and scrapbooking papers. The vellum paper used in this book belongs in this category, but variations can be found in the lightweight group as well.

Heavy weight (80 lb or greater): This group includes card stock, Canson® paper, bristol paper, and watercolor paper.

Aside from weight, physical characteristics like textures, finishes, and production methods also account for the variety of papers available today.

The texture of a sheet of paper is affected by the way in which it's produced. Machine-made paper has a more evenly spaced grain and hence a smoother surface. Handmade paper is produced by drying pulp on a screen. The beauty of the texture of a handmade sheet of paper is in not only its uneven quality but also the fact that no two sheets can ever be the same.

Uncoated and coated papers vary in their finish. A machine-made sheet of paper that has completed the final steps of the drying process is considered uncoated and has a matte appearance. Coated paper, also known as glossy paper, is treated after the drying process with a special finish (on one or both sides) that gives it sheen. It also makes it more suitable for high-density printed images such as photographs. One downside of some glossier sheets is that they are vulnerable to the appearance of fingerprints.

Recycled paper is produced with recovered waste paper and is made from material that is divided into three groups. Mill broke is paper that has never been used before. It consists of leftovers and damaged paper from a paper mill's own paper supply. Preconsumer waste is paper that has been disposed of during the manufacturing process—before being passed on to the end user. And postconsumer waste (also known as PCW) is used to create paper from material that has already served its original purpose and has been discarded by consumers. Of course you can make your own "recycled" paper. Just reuse what you already have. Make your own handmade paper or use magazines and phone books to make projects such as the Magazine Bowl (page 96), the Pod Pattern Keepsake Box (page 136), and the Bird's Nest Bowls (page 12).

Longevity is another aspect that you should consider when choosing paper for a project. If you'd like to make something that will last for a long time, use acid-free or archival-quality paper. Acid-free paper has a neutral or basic pH (7 or slightly greater). Keep this in mind when making the Filmstrip Photo Display (page 36) and Pocket Photo Album (page 116) projects.

I encourage you to mix and match and come up with your own inspired designs when choosing papers for the projects in this book. In addition, handmade papers offer a world of luxurious, inspiring options from which to choose.

To get you started as you work through the projects, here is a brief description of the main types of papers used:

- **CARD STOCK (HEAVY WEIGHT)** Card stock is a rigid type of paper with limited textures but a variety of colors and patterns. It is typically used for projects that need more rigidity and firmness.

- **BRISTOL PAPER (HEAVY WEIGHT)** Bristol paper is another rigid type of paper. It's white and is offered in two surface types. The rougher texture is well suited for use with crayons, chalks, and charcoal. The smooth finish is for working with ink. I didn't use any of these additional mediums for any embellishments of the projects, but feel free to experiment.

- **CORRUGATED CARDBOARD AND CHIPBOARD (HEAVY WEIGHT)** Corrugated cardboard and chipboard are ideal for making boxes and other projects that need to be sturdy and stand up to frequent use. Chipboard is thick pressed fiber paper that is typically made from recycled paper. It is the same type of paper found on the back of notepads. Although cardboard and chipboard are plain in color, their porous surfaces ensure strong binding with glue, and if desired, any type of paper will bond well to cover.

- **KRAFT PAPER (LIGHTWEIGHT)** Kraft paper is often made of recycled paper, and is used in different thicknesses for grocery bags, envelopes, and general packaging materials. Though not as sturdy as card stock, this paper supports projects that require greater strength than office paper. Its neutral color can be combined effectively with most other colors. This paper can be found in craft stores and office supply stores.

- **LOKTA PAPER (MEDIUM WEIGHT)** Lokta paper is more popularly known as rice paper. It's made from the bark of the *Daphne papyracea* shrub, commonly called Lokta. These plants are harvested from forests in Nepal, where workers create and dye the paper by hand, making each sheet truly unique.

- **OFFICE PAPER (LIGHTWEIGHT)** Office paper (20 lb) is the type of paper most of us commonly use in our daily lives and is often called copy or multi-purpose paper. It isn't very sturdy and can be easily folded and creased. Delicate projects such as the Fluttering Mobile (page 16) and projects that need to remain lightweight often effectively use office paper.

- **PAPYRUS (MEDIUM WEIGHT)** Papyrus was created by the ancient Egyptians and its name gives origin to the word "paper." It is believed to have been created around 4000 BC and made from the *Cyperus papyrus* plant that was once abundant in the Nile Delta in Egypt.

  Papyrus sheets are made up of thin strips of plant stalk that are positioned in a crosswise pattern. They are stronger than many modern papers of the same weight and are available in light and dark shades.

- **TISSUE PAPER (LIGHTWEIGHT)** Tissue paper is thin and translucent, and when wet, the color of the sheets will bleed. Projects that involve crumpling often incorporate tissue paper. I've used it in this book as an embellishment rather than the actual main body of a project.

- **VELLUM PAPER (MEDIUM WEIGHT)** Vellum paper is semi-translucent and low gloss. Though most commonly thought of as white, it can be found in both bright and pastel colors, as well as in marbled and metallic patterns.

Many other types of paper that are not included in the projects in this book may offer interesting alternatives, including origami paper, graph paper, newsprint, photo paper, security envelopes (with a variety of patterns on the inside), and watercolor paper. If you opt for a different paper than specified for a project, be sure to select a paper that is of similar thickness to the one listed in the materials.

TOOLS

The success of paper projects can be greatly affected by the tools that are used and how you use them.

Before you start working on a project, I recommend you find a spacious flat surface to work on, a comfortable chair, and an adequate lighting source. When you're done with your project, don't forget that your scraps can be a practical source of materials for a new project like the Bird's Nest Bowls (page 12). You never know when you may need just a small strip of a certain color or type of paper. Also, remember to clean your tools thoroughly after finishing a project. You don't want dried glue or other "leftovers" to hamper you when inspiration strikes next.

Scissors

A good pair of scissors is essential. There are all types of scissors with varying handles and blades. Find one that feels comfortable to use. I used a standard multipurpose pair of scissors with straight blades for the projects in this book. Small areas with intricate details are more easily handled with embroidery scissors.

Note For best results in papercraft, use your scissors exclusively for paper, or they will become dull quickly. Always keep the blades sharp and clean.

Craft Knife

I use my craft knife a lot. I know that it can be a little intimidating at first to use something so sharp, but with practice this tool can become a great friend. Always cut away from yourself, and for obvious reasons, keep it safely stored when not in use.

Just as with scissors, using a sharp craft knife blade for your projects is essential. There's nothing that will frustrate you more (or tear more paper) than a dull blade. You may find that some projects require more than one blade.

Sometimes I use a craft knife instead of a pencil to mark measurements on a sheet of paper. When measuring a shape to cut out, or places where a cut will not be visible, I pierce the paper with the tip of the craft knife blade. This technique simply avoids having to erase pencil markings and is especially handy when working with transparent paper, such as vellum. It is not necessary to learn how to use this technique, but with time it may be something you want to try.

Cutting Mat

A mat is required only if you're using a craft knife. Some people are comfortable cutting on a sheet of glass, but I prefer the self-healing mats. I've tried using other surfaces, but I find that a cutting mat keeps blades sharp for a long time.

Ruler

I use stainless steel rulers exclusively because I like to keep my work area simple, using only one tool when measuring and cutting with a craft knife. However, acrylic rulers, with marked lines and numbers, and T-squares can be handy to ensure accurate measurements. Use what you feel the most comfortable with.

Bone Folder

A bone folder is an essential tool for clean-looking folds and creases. It is a hand-sized, dull-edged device that looks similar to a popsicle stick. One end is tapered for use in corners and more accurate markings. It is used for marking a crease without damaging the paper. It is often carved out of the leg bone of a cow, a deer, or a similar animal, but there are synthetic alternatives as well.

Glue

The three main types of glue that I use are glue sticks, white PVA glue, and spray adhesive. The first of these three (glue sticks) dries fairly quickly and offers the thinnest coverage—reducing the possibility that the paper will warp. The second, white PVA glue, is perfect for a stronger hold, though I normally don't use it for thin papers, such as tissue paper, because the moisture of the glue makes them tear easily. Before setting paper onto white PVA glue, I like to spread out the glue evenly with an old brush. This will decrease the likelihood of bubbling or warping. Wash your brush immediately after use so that the bristles will not stiffen.

Spray adhesive is the best option when gluing large areas of paper together. Its downfall is that it isn't very forgiving. Be very sure about the placement of your paper. Once you've glued it down there is little chance you'll be able to correct any mistakes in positioning.

There are many other optional tools that you've probably seen in your favorite craft store. Scissors with fancy blades and different hole punches are just some of the things that can be used to further customize your projects. The possibilities are truly endless. However, do keep in mind that even if you have the latest and greatest tools available, mistakes will be inevitable. I still make mistakes with measurements or when cutting a shape or line. It's just something that happens and is part of the process. A good way to

avoid mistakes is to just relax and take your time.

TECHNIQUE

Scoring and folding are two techniques that any papercrafter must master. A score is basically an indentation or depression in the paper where a fold will be. These indentations allow for a crisp line when it comes time for the fold. Perfect measurements and beautiful paper can be overshadowed by improper scoring and folding.

A bone folder is essential for scoring, but there is a little trick to its proper use. I find that when scoring a sheet of paper, if a ruler is placed right on the line that needs to be scored, the thickness of the bone folder will form the indentation slightly away from the correct location. To avoid this, I place the ruler 1⁄16" (1.5mm) away from the line I'll be scoring so that the indentation will be made in the right position. This may sound minor but a poorly scored shape can lead to a crooked project. With practice you'll see where you can be more flexible with this practice. **Note** In some cases, delicate paper may not take well to the friction of an eraser, so I make sure to score and fold projects in a way that any pencil markings are hidden on the back or inside of projects.

Folding is affected by proper scoring but more importantly by the grain of the paper itself. Paper that is folded in the same direction of the grain will fold more cleanly. If a fold is made perpendicular to or against the grain, the fold will look ragged. This is much more noticeable in thicker paper. To find the direction of the grain, arch the paper as if you are going to fold it, but do not make a crease. Make note of the resistance the paper exerts. Turn the sheet 90 degrees and repeat the process. The side that offers the most resistance is the side where the grain is running against the fold. The side where you feel the least amount of resistance is where you should make your fold. If you're still not sure about the direction of the grain of your paper, crease a small sample in two different sections that are perpendicular to each other. The smoothest fold will be the one where the grain is running in the same direction as the fold.

Typically, a project will have folds in more than one direction. Once you have found the direction of the grain of your paper, make sure that you set up your project so that the majority of the folds will run along the grain of the paper. This will give your project a cleaner look.

• •

NOTE The measurements for all the projects are given as width x depth x height.

Chapter 1: Decorating

Paper is an easy, not to mention inexpensive, way to liven up any room in your home. It is very durable and can be used in many different ways. The projects in this chapter can be embellished or kept as is to fit in nicely with any other accessories that surround you. Look for paper that complements your decor, and add touches that reflect your personal flair.

One thing that I try to do with my decorating projects is to make good basic structures with solid neutral colors. I add color and texture with patterned paper in such a way that I can change it if I feel like I want a new color scheme or theme. To make it easier to change the added paper, I use double-sided tape (used in scrapbooking) or light coats of glue stick that will make it easy to remove later. There is no reason why a project has to stay the same once you've completed it.

Bird's Nest Bowls

I love these nesting bowls for several reasons but mostly because they creatively use scrap paper. They are easy to make and just happen to look stylish, too. These bowls would be terrific to make with the kids—let them choose the scraps they use. Maybe remnants from their old art projects would work.

MATERIALS

4 sheets of fuchsia heavy-weight paper, 12" (30.5cm) square, such as card stock

2 sheets of orange heavy-weight paper, 12" (30.5cm) square, such as card stock

3 sheets of red heavy-weight paper, 12" (30.5cm) square, such as card stock

Paper shredder or scissors

Glue

Water

3 nesting bowls

Brush

Cling wrap, enough to cover the outer area of the 3 bowls

FINISHED SIZE

6" x 2½" (15cm x 6.5cm)—small bowl

8" x 3½" (20.5cm x 9cm)—medium bowl

10" x 4" (25.5cm x 10cm)—large bowl

TIME: 1–2 HOURS PER BOWL

(this does not include drying time, which can take up to two days)

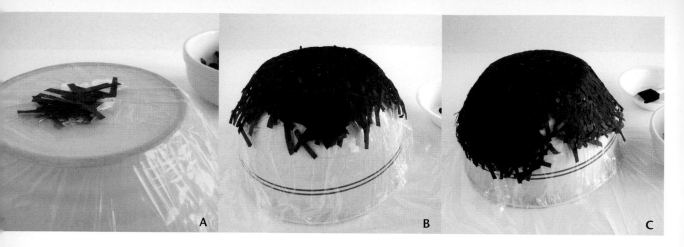

A   B   C

1 Shred the fuchsia paper using an office crosscut paper shredder. If using a regular paper shredder, cut the strips into lengths of about 1½" (3.8cm). If no paper shredder is available, use scissors to cut strips of paper that are ⅛" x 1½" (3mm x 3.8cm).

2 Prepare a solution of glue and water that is 2 parts of glue per 1 part water. Don't add too much water, or the paper will not hold together. Each bowl will require at least ½ cup (118ml) of the drippy glue solution.

3 Wrap the large bowl with cling wrap, and place it upside down on a surface covered with plastic.

4 Place the fuchsia shredded paper into another bowl, and sprinkle with some water (no more than 1 tablespoon [15ml]) to dampen the card stock.

5 Start by brushing the bottom of the cling-wrapped bowl with some of the glue solution. Add a small clump of paper (about 4–6 strips) in random fashion, and brush or dab more glue solution over them until they are damp enough that they lay flat and adhere to the bowl. **(A)**

6 Continue adding clumps of paper strips, brushing the area they will cover with the glue solution and then brushing the glue solution over them. Cover the bowl until you're about 2" (5cm) from the top edge of the bowl or the work surface. The bowl should be covered by at least 3 levels of paper to ensure stability. The edge of the bowl needs to be generally even, but keep it ragged by making some of the strips on the final row point downward, perpendicular to the work surface. **(B)**

tip*

It's important that the glue stay w enough to firmly hold the bowl together. The consistency of the 2 parts glue to 1 part water should resemble liquid soap. As you apply the glue solution, keep in mind that the more layers of paper are added the stronger the bowls will be. Allow drying time between layers.

D

Instead of using colored card stock, this is the perfect opportunity to make something out of shredded office paper. The bowls will end up looking more rustic with the different colors of paper and typographic elements on them.

Note Don't worry about covering the surface completely. Part of the charm of the bowls is to leave some small spaces, no larger than ⅛" (6mm), between some of the strips. **(C)**

7 Place the bowl in a dry and well-ventilated area, and let the surface dry completely. This process may take a day or two. If you'd like to speed it, place the bowl close to a fan. Once the surface appears dry to the touch, carefully remove the bowl from the cling wrap and let it air dry face up until the inside of the bowl is completely dry as well. **(D)**

8 Repeat the same process (steps 1–7) for the medium bowl using red paper and the smallest bowl using orange paper.

Fluttering Mobile

The artist Alexander Calder once said that when some people look at mobiles, they simply see flat objects that move, but when others look at mobiles, they see poetry. I've always fallen into the latter camp. Mobiles often are whimsical, always are fun to look at, and liven up any area in which they're placed. This project's simple repetitive folding technique makes it perfect for working on with kids. The shadows that each circular shape casts add depth and dynamism to the mobile.

MATERIALS

4 sheets of white lightweight paper, 8½" x 11" (21.5cm x 28cm), such as office paper

Scissors

1¾" (4.5cm) circle hole punch (optional)

Sewing needle

Beading monofilament

72 clear seed beads (black beads are shown in this project for better visibility)

4" (10cm) wooden embroidery hoop (the inner full circle only)

Key holder ring

FINISHED SIZE

5" x 5" x 23" (12.5cm x 12.5cm x 58.5cm)

TIME: 1–2 HOURS

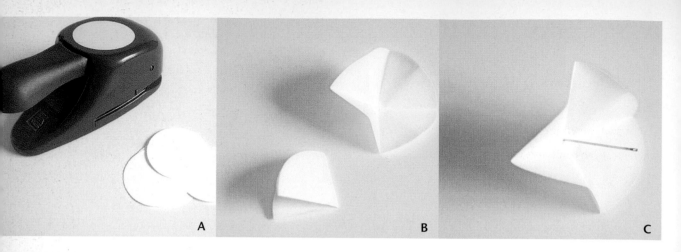

A   B   C

1 From the office paper, cut out 72 circles, each 1¾" (4.5cm) in diameter, using scissors or a hole punch. **(A)**

2 Fold each circle in half twice, then open them back up. **(B)**

3 Using the sewing needle, poke a hole in the center of each circle (at the intersection of the folds). **(C)**

4 Cut 4 strands of beading monofilament that are each 25" (63.5cm) long and 4 strands that are 21" (53.5cm) long.

5 Without using a needle, thread a bead through the first of the strands and make a simple knot around it to hold it in place. This knot will form the bottom of the monofilament strand.

6 Slide a paper circle onto the strand. Make sure that the circle opens downward.

7 Add another bead and tie a knot around it 1" (2.5cm) from the previous knot. Add a circle. Repeat this step 7 times until you have a total of 9 circles on 1 strand of monofilament. **(D)**

8 Make 7 more strands using the same process indicated in steps 5–7.

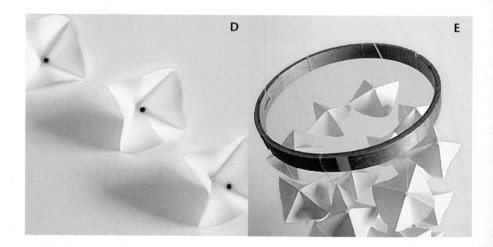

D   E

This mobile can easily be made any length. All you need to do is adjust the length of monofilament and calculate how many more (or how many fewer) circles you'll need to cut.

Note Don't worry if the circles on all the strands don't all line up perfectly. The mobile will look livelier if each of the threads is a little unevenly spaced.

9 Tie the 4 longest strands onto the wooden hoop equidistant from each other and 1" (2.5cm) from the top knot of each strand. Join the leftover length of each strand together into 1 knot. Then tie the bundle of monofilament to the key holder ring.

10 Tie the remaining strands between each of the strands already on the embroidery hoop so that the first circle on each strand hangs 1" (2.5cm) from the top knot. Make sure all the knots are secure, and cut any leftover filament. **(E)**

tip*

- *To customize this mobile's design,*
- *alternate the colors of paper circles, use*
- *textured paper, or glue a patterned paper*
- *to a solid before you begin to cut the*
- *paper into circles. You could even paint*
- *the wooden hoop to match (or contrast*
- *with) your decor.*

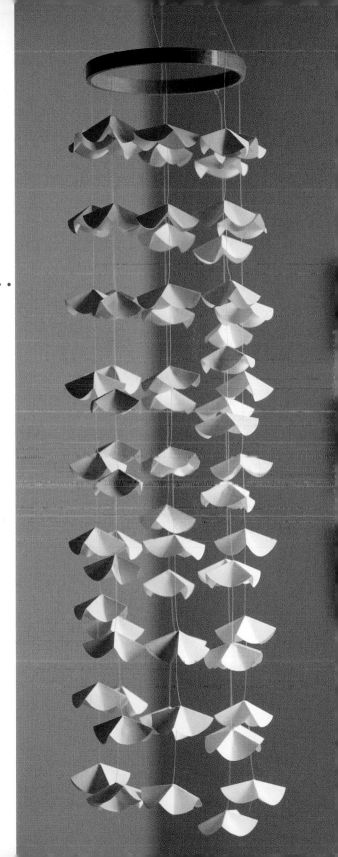

Sunburst Wreath

Throughout the ages, wreaths have symbolized many ideas, from eternal life, to strength and healing, to remembrance. For me, this Sunburst Wreath symbolizes the energy of summer and the sun's warming rays. Though we usually think about wreaths around the winter holidays, this particular wreath can be used at any time of the year—just change the color as seasons pass. This design can be worked up in a just a few hours, so consider making a group of wreaths with different sizes of embroidery hoops to make a stronger aesthetic statement or to fill up a larger wall space.

MATERIALS

4 sheets of taupe heavy-weight paper, 12" (30.5cm) square, such as card stock

Ruler

Scissors

1 embroidery hoop (only the inside ring), 10" (25.5cm) diameter

White PVA glue

Hole punch

FINISHED SIZE

17½" x 17½" (44.5cm x 44.5cm)

TIME: 2–3 HOURS . . . .

A

B

C

1 Across 1 of the sheets of card stock, cut slits that are ⅜" (9mm) apart and 11½" (29cm) long. Do not cut the strips apart; they should stay connected at 1 edge. **(A)**

2 Trim the tip of every other strip (created by the slits) 2" (5cm) shorter. The sheet will end up with a long strip on one end and a shorter strip on the other. **(B)**

3 Repeat steps 1 and 2 with two more sheets of taupe card stock.

4 Add glue to about a third of the outside of the embroidery hoop, and attach one of the slitted card stock sheets to it. The sheet should be flush to the hoop and be attached by the side that isn't cut into strips.

5 Add glue to another third of the hoop and add the second slitted sheet of card stock. Make sure the strips on the second page alternate with those on the first. For example, if you're adding a page that starts with a long strip, make sure the adjacent page ends with a short strip. **(C)**

6 Add the third slitted sheet of card stock, keeping the alternate strips rule in mind. Cut away any excess paper that overlaps.

7 Crease and fold under the upper ¼" (6mm) of each of the strips, toward the outside of the circle.

8 Add a dab of glue to the outer side of the folded tip of one strip and glue it onto the uncut opposite edge of the sheet (which is already glued to the hoop). The strip will complete a circle perpendicular to the hoop. Attach all the strips around the hoop in the same way—the shorter strips will make smaller circles. **(D)**

tip*

- *Place the wreath on a table as a centerpiece*
- *around a hurricane lamp or a group of candles.*

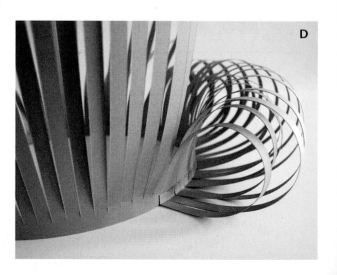

D

E

If mixing and matching fits your decor, glue lightweight sheets of paper in different colors together before cutting into strips. The wreath will be one color on the outside and allow the other color to peep through from the inside of the strips.

Note The crease of the strips will cause the loops to be leaning toward one side of the hoop—toward the front of the wreath. The side that appears flat will be the back side of the wreath and will be placed against the wall.

9 If hanging the wreath, cut a 1" x 4" (2.5cm x 5cm) rectangle out of the remaining sheet of card stock. Add glue to one side of the rectangle and fold it in half crosswise, pressing the fold together to seal. Punch a hole ½" (13mm) from the fold, centered horizontally. **(E)** Crease and fold the bottom ½" (13mm) of the tab (opposite the side of the fold),

and apply glue to the inner part of the folded tab. Attach the tab to the inside of the embroidery hoop, leaving the side with the punched hole on the back side of the wreath.

10 Cut three ½" x 12" (13mm x 30.5cm) strips of taupe card stock. Add a thin line of glue to each and use them to cover the inside of the hoop. Make sure the strips are flush to the back edge of the hoop. They are wider than the hoop in order to cover the wood. Overlap each strip ½" (13mm) over the next one until all are attached. Make sure to cover the edge of the tab that will be used for hanging the wreath. **(F)**

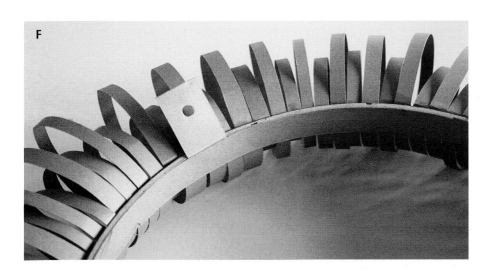

F

Shadow Forest Wall Hanging

This project takes a cue from a Japanese papercraft that emerged in the seventeenth century—the diorama, or *tatebanko*. Artists created three-dimensional scenes or landscapes using only one-dimensional pieces of paper, at times enclosing them in a kind of paper shadow box. The most important lesson to learn from diorama techniques is that modifying the scale of objects helps to reinforce perceived depth. Smaller objects should always be placed in the layer closest to the back, and the larger objects should be toward the front. This is called an open diorama.

The shapes used in this wall hanging are silhouettes and include only basic features of the trees. It's all you need to evoke the image. I've designed this wall hanging to be hung so that its construction can be a part of its appeal; however, if you prefer a more polished look, you can set this wall hanging in a frame.

MATERIALS

3 sheets of letter-sized tracing paper, 8½" x 11" (21.5cm x 28cm)

Soft pencil

1 sheet of dark green heavy-weight paper, 8½" x 11" (21.5cm x 28cm), such as card stock

1 sheet of light green heavy-weight paper, 8½" x 11" (21.5cm x 28cm), such as card stock

1 sheet of white heavy-weight paper, 8½" x 11" (21.5cm x 28cm), such as card stock

Craft knife

Ruler

Cutting mat

White PVA glue

4 balsa wood sticks, 7" x ⅜" x ⅜" (18cm x 1cm x 1cm) each

Saw-tooth picture hanger with nails

Hammer

FINISHED SIZE

7" x 11" x ¾" (18cm x 28cm x 2cm)

TIME: 1–2 HOURS . . . .

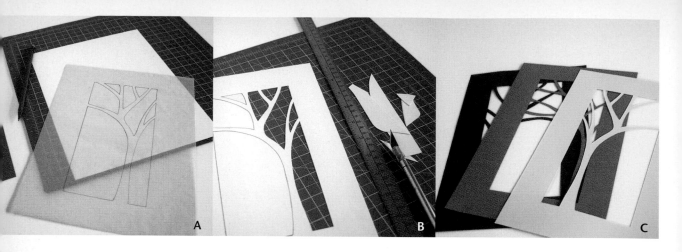

A

B

C

1 Copy the 3 templates on the facing page at 200 percent, and trace each one of them onto tracing paper with a soft pencil. (A)

2 Center the 3 tracings, with each facing down onto the corresponding card stock, and retrace. The tracings will be transferred by the pressure of the pencil. Template A should be transferred onto the white card stock; template B should be transferred onto the light green card stock; and template C should be transferred onto the dark green card stock.

3 Cut out the negative space around the trees using a craft knife. Make sure to use a ruler to help keep the edges straight for a clean look. (B), (C)

4 Lightly glue one balsa stick along the top and another along the bottom borders of the front of the dark green card stock. The stick edges should be flush with the edges of the card stock. (D)

5 Glue the light green card stock (right side up) to the balsa sticks, and glue the remaining 2 balsa sticks along the top and bottom borders of the light green card stock, directly on top of the previous set of sticks. (E)

6 Glue the white card stock (right side up) to the last set of balsa sticks. (F)

7 Center and use the hammer to nail the saw-tooth hanger onto the top back of the entire piece (nail through the card stock and into the balsa sticks). (G)

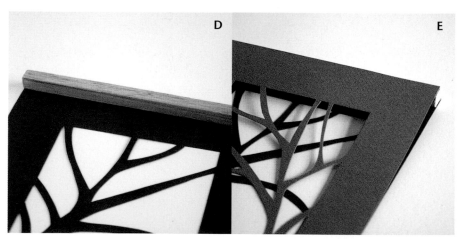

D

E

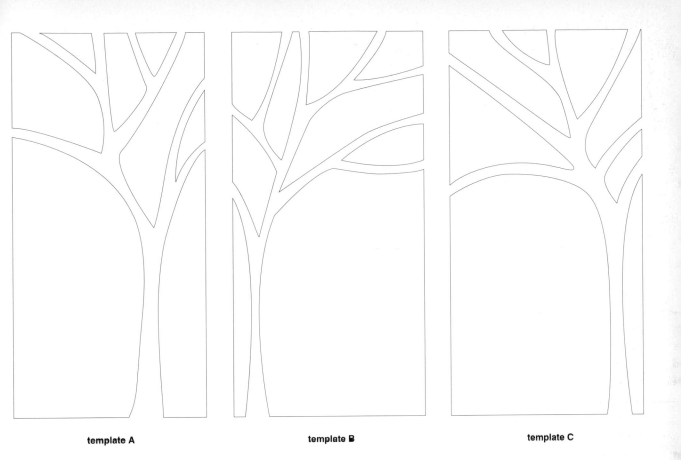

template A   template B   template C

F

G

Tropical Flower

This flower will instantly add a little burst of nature-inspired decoration to any table or wall niche. And, it's the perfect way to brighten a dark corner where plants can't be placed. For entertaining, coordinate the colors of the petals and the base to match your decor, and place several of these flowers together on the table for an attractive centerpiece display. They can be either the same height and used in a straight row or of varying heights and clustered as a group. Or, use a larger wooden base and "plant" several flowers in the same "pot." Just make sure when you are drilling the holes to account for the width of each flower.

MATERIALS

1 wooden cube, 3½" (9cm)

Drill and 5⁄16" (8mm) drill bit

1 small foam brush

1 wooden dowel, 5⁄16" x 13" (8mm x 33cm)

Wood stain

White PVA glue

1 strip of white lightweight paper, 2" x 4" (5cm x 10cm), such as office paper

Scissors

1 sheet of pink heavy-weight paper, 18" (45.5cm) square, such as card stock

Self-adhesive transparent tape, such as Scotch® tape

1 strip of white lightweight paper, 1" x 3" (2.5cm x 7.5cm), such as office paper

FINISHED SIZE

3½" x 3½" x 13" (9cm x 9cm x 33cm)

TIME: 2–3 HOURS . . . .

A

B

C

1 Drill a hole that is at least 1" (2.5cm) deep into the center of one side of the wooden cube. **(A)**

2 Using the foam brush, paint the wooden dowel and the cube with the wood stain.

3 When both the dowel and the cube are dry, dab glue onto one end of the dowel and insert that end into the drilled hole.

4 Cut slits across the entire long side of the 2" x 4" (5cm x 10cm) strip of white paper. The slits should measure at least 1" (2.5cm) deep and be spaced ⅛" (3mm) apart from one another.

5 Dab a bit of glue around the tip of the dowel opposite the cube, and wrap a third of the white strip of paper around it. The fringed slits should point upward. **(B), (C)**

6 For the flower's petals, cut 1 oval out of the pink card stock that is 4" (10cm) long and 1" (2.5cm) at its widest point. The

oval should have tapered ends, not rounded tips. Use this petal as a template to trace and cut out 14 additional petals from the card stock.

7 Draw and cut a larger, similarly shaped petal out of the card stock. This petal should measure 5½" (14cm) long and 1¾" (4.5cm) at its widest point. Use this petal as a template to trace and cut out 14 additional petals.

8 To assemble the flower, center and attach a 1½" (3.8cm) length of tape perpendicular to one end of a shorter petal. The tape should overlap the petal by ¼" (6mm). Hold the petal in a vertical position next to the dowel, and wrap the tape around the base of the white strip of paper on the

D

E

F

dowel. The base of the petal and the white strip should be at the same height. This petal will form part of the first ring of flower petals.

9 Tape 3 more short petals, evenly spaced, to the dowel using the same attachment procedure. **(D)**

10 Add another ring of 4 short petals at the same height on the dowel, spacing them between the petals in the first ring.

11 Continue taping the remainder of the short petals to the dowel in rings, alternating their spacing between petals from the previous ring. **(E)**

12 Curl the remaining long petals outward by wrapping them around a pencil before they are attached to the stem. Attach these petals in an evenly spaced spiral form that slowly descends along the dowel.

Note As you add the petals, look at the flower from the top and from the side to make sure the distribution of petals is even.

13 Wrap the ¼" (6mm) wide strip of white paper around the base of the flower to cover all the tape. Seal the end with a bit of glue. **(F)**

Arizona Lamp

There's just something I adore about the Southwest, with its warm terra-cotta colors and spicy flavors. This stylish lamp evokes the Arizona desert at sunset, and a cozy corner can be created with its indirect light (maybe add some wildflowers in a low vase nearby). In this case, the light beam shines upward, and the vellum softens its glow. Make assembly easy by using a puck light, a light typically placed under kitchen cabinets.

MATERIALS

1 sheet of brown medium-weight paper, 20" x 30" (51cm x 76cm), such as Lokta paper

Ruler

Scissors

Hole punch

Spray adhesive

1 sheet of white medium-weight paper, 23" x 12" (58.5cm x 30.5cm), such as thick vellum paper

Bone folder

1 puck light

Drill

1 square piece of wood, 5" x 5" x ½" (12.5cm x 12.5cm x 13mm)

White PVA glue

Glue stick

FINISHED SIZE

5" x 5" x 12" (12.5cm x 12.5cm x 30.5cm) . . . .

TIME: 30 MINUTES–1 HOUR

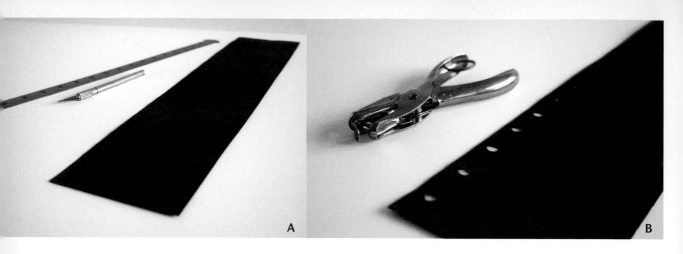

A

B

1 Measure and cut a 21" x 4" (53.5cm x 14cm) strip of brown paper. **(A)**

2 Draw a line that is ½" (13mm) from the edge of the long side of the brown paper.

3 Punch 1 hole every 1" (2.5cm), aligning the bottom of each hole with the line drawn in step 2. **(B)**

4 Using the spray adhesive, glue the brown paper over the vellum. The short sides of both sheets should be flush, and the long side of the brown paper without holes should be flush with a long side of the vellum. The punched holes will face toward the center of the vellum.

5 Measure, score, and fold 4 vertical lines (parallel to the shortest end of the 2 glued sheets) at 3" (7.5cm), 8" (20.5cm), 13" (33cm), and 18" (45.5cm). **(C)**

tip*

Make a more elaborate design by punching holes in the vellum with a push pin or with hole punches like those typically used for scrapbooking, available in varying sizes.

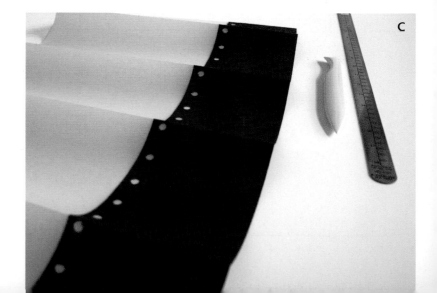

C

Adjust the height of the lamp to suit your space by gluing the brown paper to a wider or narrower piece of vellum in step 4. When you do so, hide any pencil markings that you've made by facing the marked sides in toward each other before gluing down.

6 Following the manufacturer's instructions, attach the puck light to the center of the wood board. This board will become the base of your lamp. Make sure that the cable extends off the center of one of the sides of the base. **(D)**

7 Measure and cut a ¾" (2cm) square out of each of the sheet's 2 bottom corners (the long side covered with the brown paper).

8 Place the wooden base on a flat surface, apply a thin line of white glue around the outer ½" (13mm) edge of the board, and wrap the paper around the square, making sure that the folds made in step 5 match up with each of the 4 corners of the base. Before gluing down, note that the short ends of the vellum will overlap by ½" (13mm). Center this overlap on the side of the base from which the puck light cable extends. The cable should be placed through the cutouts made in step 7. **(E)**

9 Use the glue stick to glue the overlapped sections of vellum together. Do not use too much glue or the vellum will warp.

D

E

Filmstrip Photo Display

Not many of us capture memories on a true filmstrip anymore (or even on film!), but we still tend to record our lives according to a timeline. The three-dimensional Filmstrip Photo Display is the perfect way to tell the story of precious memories without saying a word. Maybe you've captured the ever-changing facial expressions of your favorite infant or the moments before, during, and after a special event. Make two or more of these displays to make a large impact on a wall and, of course, show off more photos. This is an effective way to visually tell the story of a family event or outing with friends. And, the frame's construction makes it easy to switch the photographs from behind the frame, so you can change your design as often as you print your pictures.

MATERIALS

1 sheet of white heavy-weight paper, 11" x 15½" (28cm x 39.5cm), such as acid-free card stock

1 letter-sized sheet of the same white heavy-weight paper, 8½" x 11" (21.5cm x 28cm), such as card stock

1 sheet of black heavy-weight paper, 11" x 15½" (28cm x 39.5cm), such as card stock

Scissors

Ruler

Hole punch

Glue stick

Bone folder

FINISHED SIZE

9" x 15½" x 1½" (23cm x 39.5cm x 3.8cm)

TIME: 1–2 HOURS . . . .

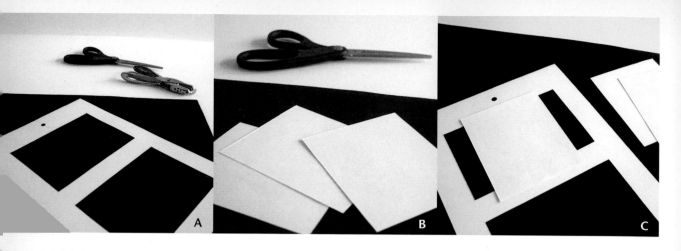

1 Measure and cut a 9" x 15½" (23cm x 39.5cm) sheet from the larger sheet of white card stock.

2 Punch a hole at the top of the white sheet, centered and ¾" (2cm) from the edge of the short end. This will become the top of the frame.

3 Measure and cut three 5" x 3½" (12.5cm x 9cm) rectangles that are centered between the side of the page, 1½" (3.8cm) from the top of the sheet and 1" (2.5cm) away from each other. **(A)**

4 Cut the letter-sized sheet of white card stock into 3 pieces that each measure 3½" x 4½" (9cm x 11.5cm). **(B)**

5 Add glue along only the top and bottom ¼" (6mm) of the short ends of the 3 sheets of paper, and center 1 on the back of each of the openings. Make sure that you are gluing them to the side of the large white sheet that has the pencil markings that were made when measuring the openings. A photo should comfortably slide in between the newly added piece of paper and the larger sheet. **(C)**

6 To make the "filmstrip" for the frame, measure and score ½" (13mm) from each of the long edges of the black card stock. Make sure to crease the card stock with the bone folder.

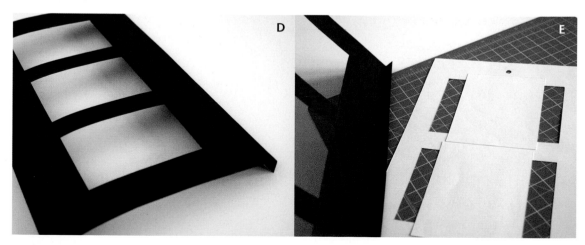

Since you are thinking in three dimensions, why not show off small, lightweight objects instead of just photos? Simply glue your treasures to the back sheet to show them off. Want to switch things up? Just remove the back sheet and replace it with a new one.

7 Measure and cut three 4" x 3½" (10cm x 9cm) rectangles that are centered between the sides of the black card stock, 1½" (3.8cm) from the top of the sheet and 1" (2.5cm) away from each other. **(D)**

8 Place the black card stock onto the white sheet, aligning the openings, fold the black sheet's folded edges to the back of the white sheet, and glue the folded edges down. **(E), (F)**

tip*

Though most paper used today has a long "shelf life," when creating projects to display photography, it's best to use acid-free paper to preserve the color and counteract the natural deterioration of paper over time. Manufacturers often apply a chemical base to the paper to neutralize the naturally occurring acids in the wood pulp—resulting in a paper that will better protect your cherished photographs.

Light as Air
Floating Cubby

This cubby provides an elegant alternative for displaying small objects when shelf space is not available. Choose background and frame colors according to the decor of your room and to complement the items the cubby will hold; group a collection of these cubbies to make a striking statement. Because this project uses card stock, these cubbies can hold small light-weight items only. To create a floating cubby capable of supporting heavier items (still under 2 pounds), you can substitute cardboard or chipboard for the cardstock. Just be sure to allow extra drying time if you cover the cardboard with decorative paper (page 8).

MATERIALS

- 1 sheet of white heavy-weight paper, 12" x 12" (30.5cm x 30.5cm), such as card stock

- 1 sheet of white heavy-weight paper, 8½" x 11" (21.5cm x 28cm), such as card stock

- 2 reinforcement rings

- 1 sheet of brown textured heavy-weight paper, 12" x 12" (30.5cm x 30.5cm), such as card stock

Pencil

Scissors

Ruler

White PVA glue

Bone folder

FINISHED SIZE

10" x 10" x 2" (25.5cm x 25.5cm x 5cm)

TIME: 1–2 HOURS . . . .

A   B   C

1 Measure and draw a 6" (15cm) square in the center of the 12" (30.5cm) square white sheet.

2 Measure and draw 1 rectangle that is 2" x 6" (5cm x 15cm) above the square and 1 of the same dimensions below the square. The rectangles should be adjacent to the square, each sharing a long side with one of the square's sides.

3 Measure and draw 2 additional rectangles, each measuring 1" x 6" (2.5cm x 15cm), 1 above and 1 below the rectangles drawn in step 2. These rectangles should be adjacent to the previous ones.

4 Turn the sheet of paper 90 degrees, and repeat steps 2 and 3. **(A)**

5 Draw a small rectangle measuring 1" x 2" (2.5cm x 5cm) to the left and another to the right of each rectangle that is adjacent to the center square; you will draw 4 of these rectangles in total.

6 Following the outermost line, cut out the entire shape.

7 Cut through the 1" (2.5cm) part of the rectangles drawn in step 5 that keeps them attached to the main piece. Then cut the 2 exposed corners of each of the rectangles on a diagonal to turn them into tabs. **(B)**, **(C)**

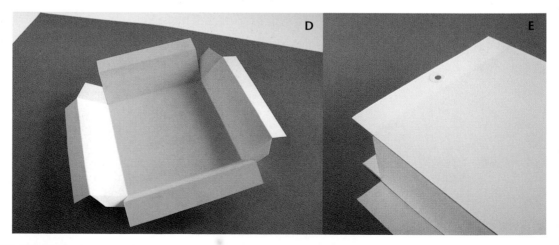

D   E

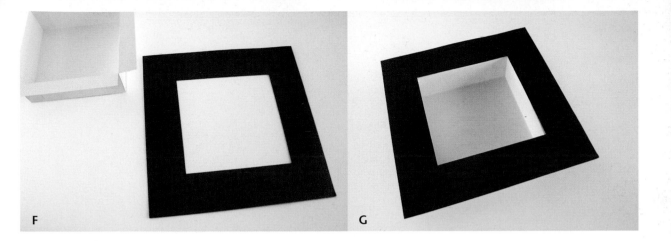

F

G

8 Using the bone folder, score and crease the square and rectangles as shown in the photo. Make sure that all the pencil markings are left on the back. **(D)**

9 Glue the tabs to the outer sides of the cubby.

10 Measure, draw, and cut a 6" x 7" (15cm x 18cm) rectangle out of the smaller white sheet of card stock. Punch a hole centered at the top of the shorter edge and ½" (13mm) from the edge of the sheet. Add a reinforcement ring to the front and another to the back of the hole.

11 Glue this smaller sheet to the back of the cubby, making sure the bottom edges of both line up. The top of the smaller sheet (where the hole is) should hang over the edge of the cubby. **(E)**

12 Cut the brown card stock down to a 10" (25.5cm) square. From its center point, measure, draw, and cut out a 6" (15cm) square. **(F)**

14 Glue the brown sheet of card stock to the front of the white cubby, centering the opening of the brown square over the cubby. **(G)**

Papercraft Secret: Cutting Corners

Tabs are commonly used to attach 2 sides that are perpendicular to one another. They help make an object sturdier, and for the projects in this book, they are used to create boxes. The outer 2 corners are always cut on an angle so that no extra paper interferes with a sharp and accurate box corner.

tip*

Once you've assembled the cubby, trim

the edges with decorative-edged scissors

or add a pattern with a hole punch to

change the look from minimal to ornate.

Stair-Step Mirror

Mirrors are such a resourceful solution to brighten up a corner or a hallway. They can also make a room look larger. My favorite part of this design is the fact that even though only one color of paper is used, the shadows make it seem like there are two different types of paper. The crisp scoring and folding are what really make this design complete.

MATERIALS

Craft knife

Cutting mat

Ruler

Pencil

1 sheet of foam board, 20" x 30" x ³⁄₁₆" (51cm x 76cm x 5mm)

Scissors

3 sheets of orange medium-weight paper, 18" x 18"
    (45.5cm x 45.5cm), such as card stock

Spray adhesive

Glue stick

Universal adhesive or glue

1 mirror, 8" x 8" (20.5cm x 20.5cm)

Bone folder

FINISHED SIZE

16" x 16" x 1" (40.5cm x 40.5cm x 2.5cm)

TIME: 3–4 HOURS . . . .

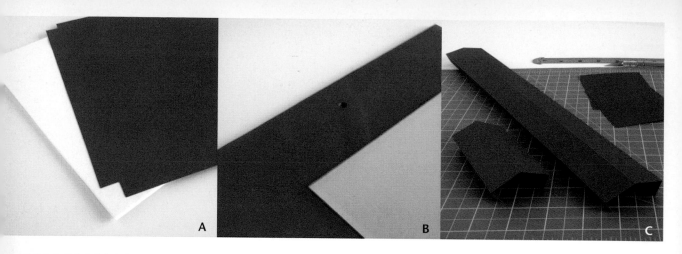

A   B   C

1 Using a craft knife, cut a 16" (40.5cm) square out of the foam board.

2 Cut an 18" (45.5cm) square of orange card stock, then center and glue it on the foam board, using the spray adhesive. Cut 1" (2.5cm) squares out of each of the 4 corners of the card stock. Use the excess orange card stock to wrap the edges of the foam board, then glue them to the back of the board using the glue stick. **(A)**

3 Using the craft blade, make a hole that goes through the paper and the foam core, that is at least ½" (13mm) wide, centered, and 1½" (3.8cm) from the top edge of the square.

4 Using the universal glue, center and attach the mirror to the orange side of the foam board. **(B)**

5 Cut four 16" x 3" (40.5cm x 7.5cm) strips of orange card stock and eight that measure 4" x 3" (10cm x 7.5cm).

6 Score and fold all of the strips in half lengthwise. Open up the strips.

7 Measure, score, and fold ½" (13mm) of each long edge toward the central fold on each strip. These folded-under edges will be the tabs used to glue the strips to the mirror frame. **(C)**

tip*

> *To achieve a brightly colored*
>
> *mirror, use alternating col-*
>
> *ors of paper for each of the*
>
> *horizontal shapes.*

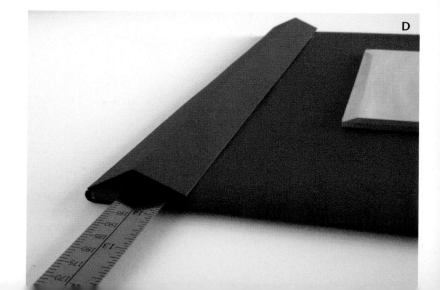

D

E

8 Make small markings every 2" (5cm) on the left and right edges of the foam board.

9 Prepare to assemble the frame by setting the edge of a long strip lengthwise, flush with the top of the foam board. The strip should form a pitched triangle shape, with the bottom edge aligned with the first set of 2" (5cm) markings on the board's edge. Tuck the tabs under the triangle shape at the ends of the strip, and use the glue stick to attach them to the top of the foam board. If needed, slide a ruler on either side of the strip and inside the raised part of it to press the tabs against the board. **(D)**

10 Glue a second long strip to the foam board. The top edge should touch the bottom of the first strip, and the bottom edge should touch the top of the mirror.

11 On each side of the mirror, glue the 4 short strips of scored card stock every 2" (5cm). Remember that the tabs should be neatly tucked under each one of the strips. **(E)**

12 Glue the 2 remaining longer strips in the same way from the bottom of the mirror to the bottom edge of the foam board.

Before hanging the finished mirror on the wall, check that the mirror has been very securely glued in step 4 and always use an adhesive that is appropriate for gluing glass on paper, or prop the mirror directly on a shelf (as shown in the photo on page 44).

Infinity Cube Wall Art

Here's an exciting opportunity to produce your own wall art in the style of M. C. Escher. This project is just the thing for someone who prefers contemporary shapes as part of their decor. I used two contrasting colors of paper to create a focal point in the center of the design, but adding multiple colors and patterns will radically change its effect. How about making a colorful patchwork quilt or even bubbles floating in the sky? What about mimicking the vibrant display in a kaleidoscope?

MATERIALS

1 sheet of tracing paper, 8½" x 11" (21.5cm x 28cm)

Pencil

3 sheets of white heavy-weight paper, 12" (30.5cm) square, such as card stock

1 sheet of orange heavy-weight paper, 8½" x 11" (21.5cm x 28cm), such as card stock

Bone folder

Ruler

White PVA glue

Black shadow box frame, 10" x 10" x 1¾" (25.5cm x 25.5cm x 4.5cm)

FINISHED SIZE

10" x 10" x 1¾" (25.5cm x 25.5cm x 4.5cm)—includes frame dimensions

TIME: 1–2 HOURS.

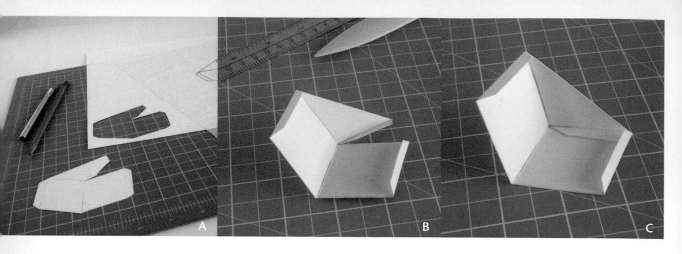

A   B   C

1 Copy the template below. Trace the template with a soft pencil. Flip the tracing paper over, and retrace 6 times onto the white card stock and 1 time onto the orange card stock. Cut out all 7 tracings. **(A)**

2 Score and fold all 7 pieces, making sure that all pencil outlines are on the inside of each shape. **(B)**

3 Add glue to the front side of the tab attached to the triangle on 1 of the cutouts, and glue it to the underside of the nearest parallelogram. Repeat the same process for the other 6 cutouts. **(C)**

4 Measure and cut a 9" (23cm) square out of a sheet of white card stock.

5 Apply glue to the 2 tabs on the right and left sides of the orange half cube, and glue it to the center of the large white card stock. Make sure that the triangle is at the top and that the parallelograms are on the right and left sides of the half cube.

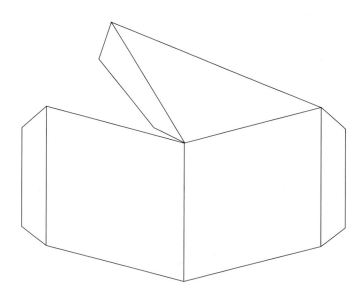

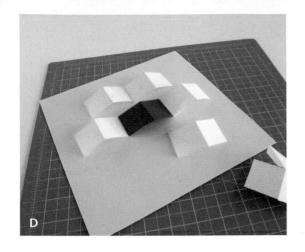

D

tip*

Play with the placement of the blocks before gluing them down. You may prefer lining them up differently or placing them in a tighter configuration. Experiment! Use a larger shadow box frame to allow more cubes to be added to the pattern.

6 Glue 2 white half cubes adjacent to the right and left sides of the orange half cube.

7 Glue 2 of the remaining white half cubes ½" (13mm) above the center row, aligning the points of these half cubes with the valleys between those in the center row. **(D)**

8 Glue the remaining 2 half cubes ½" (13mm) below the center row, again aligning their points with the valleys in the center row. **(E)**

9 When the glue is dry, insert the card stock in the shadow box frame.

E

Mod Wall Clock

Flower power! It still amazes me when just a few pieces of paper can make such a unique and complicated looking project. And it's so functional. With the help of a basic clock mechanism I was able to create this whimsical clock with just 3 pieces of paper. The style of the clock will change with your choices of paper color, and you can easily make this a larger or smaller clock, depending on the wall space available to you.

MATERIALS

1 sheet of tracing paper, 11" x 17" (28cm x 43cm)

Pencil

2 sheets of white heavy-weight paper, 18" (45.5cm) square, such as card stock

Scissors

Craft knife

Cutting mat

1 sheet of dark gray heavy-weight paper, 18" (45.5cm) square, such as card stock

1 foam board, 20" x 30" (51cm x 76cm)

Glue stick

Clock mechanism with silver clock hands, ¼" (6mm) shaft

Hole punch, ½" (13mm) in diameter

Hole punch, ¼" (6mm) in diameter

FINISHED SIZE

15" x 15" x 1½" (38cm x 38cm x 3.8cm)

TIME: 2–3 HOURS

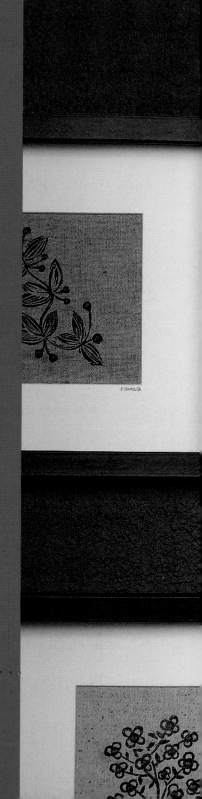

1 Copy the template on the facing page at 300 percent. Trace the template with a soft pencil, and place the tracing paper face down on 1 sheet of white card stock. Retrace the design so that the image is transferred on to the white card stock. Cut around the outline of the design with scissors, and use a craft knife to cut out the 4 crescent shapes (the petals of the clock) and the ¼" (6mm) circle in the center. **(A)**

2 Use the cut white card stock as a template, and trace the outer shape onto the second sheet of white card stock, the sheet of gray card stock, and the piece of foam board. Do not trace the 4 crescent shapes, but do trace the small circle in the center. Cut along the outline made on each sheet of card stock. Don't forget to cut out the circle in the center of each sheet.

3 Cut the foam board ⅛" (3mm) smaller than the drawn outline. Then, cut along the inner circle, using a pencil to poke through the cut piece.

4 Center and glue the foam board onto the back of the sheet of white card stock that does not have crescent cutouts.

5 Center the gray card stock on the back of the foam board, rotate it about 10 degrees counterclockwise, and then glue the 2 pieces together.

Note The top petal of these sheets will be in the 12 o'clock position.

tip*

- *To customize the clock to your decor, use patterned paper in place of the gray card stock for the back of the clock.*
- *Then pick out one of the colors used in the patterned paper to create the clock hands. If you choose to change the*
- *color of the face of the clock (which is white in this version), I recommend you select a solid color. Otherwise the clock*
- *hands may be hard to see.*

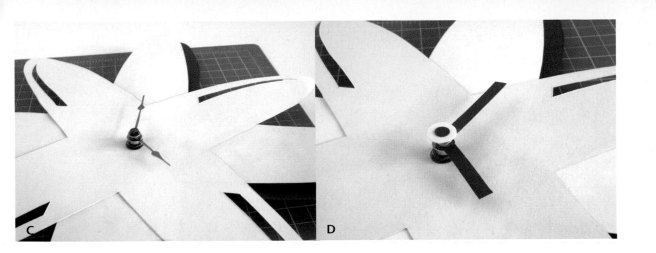

C

D

. . . .

6 Center the white card stock with the crescent cutouts on the front of the white card stock that is attached to the foam board, at a 45-degree angle or in an X position. Glue the 2 pieces together. **(B)**

7 Insert the clock mechanism into the hole through the back of the foam board and all the card stock. Attach the clock hands to the clock mechanism. **(C)**

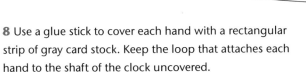

8 Use a glue stick to cover each hand with a rectangular strip of gray card stock. Keep the loop that attaches each hand to the shaft of the clock uncovered.

9 Attach the clock handles to the shaft that juts through the front of the clock, following the manufacturer's instructions.

10 Punch a circle out of white card stock that is ½" (13mm) in diameter and one out of gray card stock that is ¼" (6mm). Glue the white circle centered over the shaft. Glue the gray circle centered over the white one. **(D)**

Ripple Frame

Create a "ripple" of interest with this visually intriguing frame that will highlight your photograph without overpowering it. The most important part of this project is to make sure that all the strips used for the rolls are of the same exact width. If the measurements are inaccurate, the rolls won't line up properly. Call attention to colors within your chosen photograph by choosing a complementary or similarly colored paper. Then cut 1" (2.5cm) strips of paper that are one-quarter the width of the rolls. Glue and wrap the strips around the center of each roll or at either end.

MATERIALS

3 sheets of turquoise heavy-weight paper, 12" (30.5cm) square, such as card stock

Ruler

Scissors

Smooth round pencil

White PVA glue

Paintbrush

1 wooden frame, 5" x 7" (12.5cm x 18cm), designed for 4" x 6" (10cm x 15cm) photos

FINISHED SIZE

5" x 7" x ¾" (12.5cm x 18cm x 2cm)

TIME: 30 MINUTES–1 HOUR . . . .

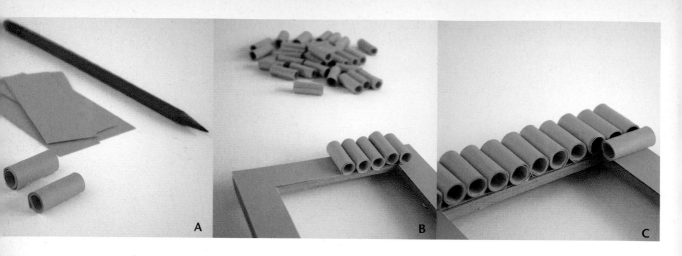

A

B

C

1 Measure and cut out 54 strips of turquoise card stock that are 1" x 3½" (2.5cm x10cm).

2 Wrap each strip into a tight roll around the pencil. Seal each roll with a dab of glue. **(A)**

3 Cut out a turquoise card stock frame that is 5" x 7" (12.5cm x 18cm) and has an opening that is 3¼" x 5¼" (8.25cm x 13.3cm), the same size as the wooden frame's opening, and glue it to the face of the wooden frame, smoothing the glue with a paintbrush before pressing the paper onto the frame.

4 Mark the center of the top and the bottom of the frame. Align rolls to the right and to the left of each of the markings on the top and bottom of the frame, perpendicular to the frame's edge. Place a bead of glue along each roll,

making sure the seams where the ends of the strips were glued face down against the frame and are hidden from view. Set each roll into place on the frame. The rolls should all be vertical and will probably hang slightly over the edge of the frame. **(B)**

5 Glue the remaining rolls of paper to the sides of the frame in a horizontal position. **(C), (D)**

The paper rolls used in this project can also be used to decorate the surfaces of other items, such as the frame of a mirror or the outer part of a napkin ring.

tip*

I designed this project for a 5" x 7" (12.5cm x 18cm) frame that accommodates 4" x 6" (10cm x 15cm) photographs. However, the technique learned here can be applied to frames of other sizes. Measure, cut, and roll the paper as you would in steps 1–3. Then, arrange the rolls in different vertical and horizontal combinations until you find the pattern that works best for the dimensions of your frame.

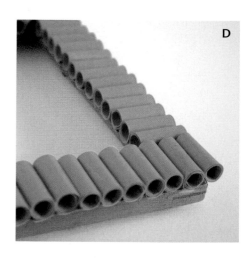

D

With a bit of planning and some time, you can welcome your guests with unique table settings and decorations that will highlight your personal sense of style. Colorful paper options abound that can set an instant festive mood for your event. Most of these paper projects can be reused, and small modifications can be made to update them for future gatherings.

I like using paper projects for entertaining because I can customize them to my own liking. Often, I can't find exactly what I'm looking for in stores, or the paper products that I do like are too expensive. A great way to save your time and budget is to purchase solid- or neutral-tone paper goods that you can embellish yourself. For example, the paper flower made for the Flower Favor Box (page 128) can be added to a napkin ring, to a place card, or to any other items that are part of your event; the flowers used on the Box Flower String Lights (page 78) can also be added to a napkin ring (maybe with a button in the middle). There are many ways you can adapt your own ideas to pre-made paper goods. The options are as limitless as your imagination.

Pillar Tealight Cover

Tealights can lend a sensational atmosphere to any type of gathering. They're low enough that guests can see each other during dinner conversation, and they're compact enough that they won't take too much space. Use these tealight covers to dress up a dinner table or add some romantic lighting to a party.

MATERIALS

2 sheets of medium-weight paper, 11" x 17" (28cm x 43cm), such as vellum paper

Pencil

Scissors

Eraser

Compass

1 sheet of foam board, 20" x 30" (51cm x 76cm)

Craft knife

Cutting mat

White PVA glue

Blue heavy-weight paper, 18" (45.5cm) square, such as card stock

Tealight candle and small glass votive

FINISHED SIZE

5" x 9" x 5" (12.5cm x 23cm x 12.5cm)

TIME: 1–2 HOURS

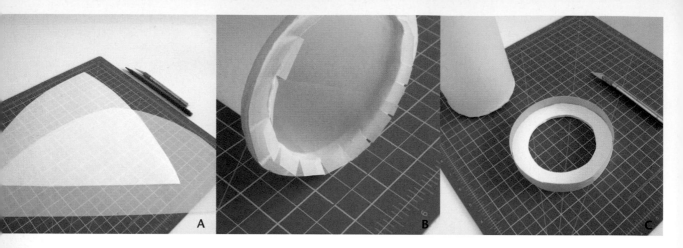

A   B   C

1 Copy the templates on the facing page at 300 percent, and trace very lightly onto each of the vellum sheets (1 template per sheet).

2 Cut along the outline of each tracing, and erase any leftover pencil markings. **(A)**

3 Using the compass, draw a ring on the foam board with an outer diameter of 4" (10cm) and an inner diameter of 3¼" (9.5cm). Cut out the ring with the craft knife. Make sure that your blade is very sharp.

4 Curl the largest sheet of vellum (template B) into a cylinder, and glue its outer rim to the inside edge of the ring, making sure the bottom of the vellum extends ¼" (6mm) past the ring's bottom edge.

5 Using the scissors, cut slits on the vellum that extend past the edge of the ring. The slits should be perpendicular to the ring and spaced ½" (13mm) apart, creating tabs. **(B)**

tip *

- *Never place this cover over an open flame. Make*
- *sure that your tealight candle is always in a votive*
- *or small glass.*

6 Fold over and glue the tabs to the underside of the ring.

7 Curl the smallest sheet of vellum (template A) into a cylinder, and glue its inner rim to the outside edge of the ring, again leaving ½" (13mm) of vellum past the edge. The tapered point of the vellum should be on the opposite side from the tapered point of the first sheet of vellum.

8 Repeat steps 5 and 6 for the second sheet of vellum. On the underside of the ring, the tabs of the second sheet of vellum should be folded over the tabs of the first sheet of vellum.

9 Using the compass, draw another ring on the foam core with an outer diameter of 5" (12.5cm) and an inner diameter of 3¼" (9.5cm). Cut out the ring with the craft knife.

10 Measure and cut out a strip of blue card stock that is ¾" x 17½" (2cm x 44.5cm).

11 Glue the blue strip of paper around the outer edge of larger ring, making sure that it is flush to one side of the ring. **(C)**

12 Center and glue the ring with the blue paper (flush side to the bottom) to the bottom of the ring with the vellum paper. **(D)**

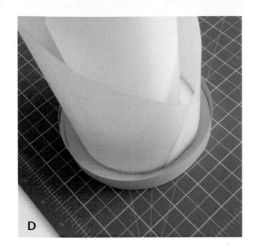

D

• •

13 Place the tealight cover over a tealight candle that is (for safety purposes) inside a small glass votive.

The blue strip of card stock at the base of the cover can be replaced by any colorful length of ribbon or patterned paper.

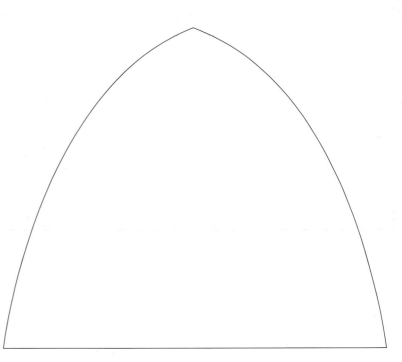

template A

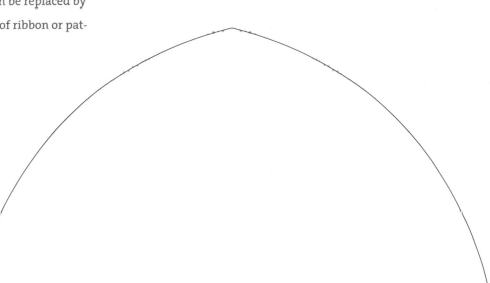

template B

Mosaic Place Mats

Mosaic art, which first appeared many centuries ago, is made with small pieces of glass, stone, tiles, or other materials. The mosaic design of these place mats is inspired by this tradition but is worked in reverse—cutting pieces of paper out instead of adding them. The colors of the green paper and of the table itself provide contrast and interest. While the front of the place mats can be made the same for all the place settings, consider changing which shapes are cut out of the colored background paper to create variety at the table.

   Though this place mat design whips up in a flash, you can always save time by skipping steps 4–6 and substituting an uncut multicolored piece of paper for the green background.

MATERIALS

2 sheets of tracing paper

Soft pencil

4 sheets of 2-ply binder's board of .04" (1mm) thickness, 13" x 19" (33cm x 48.5cm)

Craft knife

Cutting mat

1 sheet of green medium-weight paper, 20" x 30" (51cm x 76cm), such as Lokta paper

Glue stick

FINISHED SIZE

11½" x 16½" (29cm x 42 cm)

TIME: 1–2 HOURS

(to make 4 place mats)

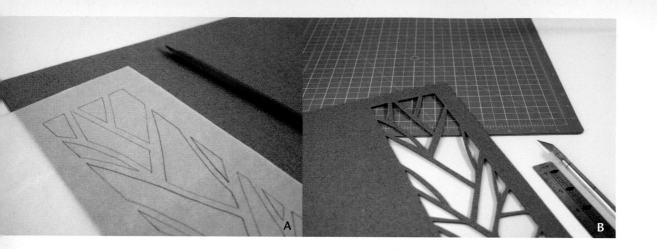

A

B

1 Copy the template on the facing page at 137 percent. On tracing paper, trace over the template with a soft pencil. **(A)**

2 Place the tracing paper onto a sheet of binder's board (drawing side down), and center the drawing 1" (2.5cm) from the edge of the left-hand shorter side of the board. Retrace the drawing to transfer it to the board. The side on which the drawing is traced will become the back of the place mat.

3 Using the craft knife and the cutting mat, cut out the negative spaces (including those shaded gray on the template) of the drawing from the board. **(B)**

4 Use the board from step 3 as a template to trace the leaf pattern onto each remaining sheet of binder's board. Then cut out the negative spaces of each drawing.

tip *

- *If you'd like a more elaborate*
- *design, repeat the rectangular*
- *pattern on both the right and*
- *left sides of the place mats.*

5 Cut 4 strips of green paper that measure 4" x 12" (10cm x 30.5cm).

6 Center the tracing used in step 1 face down over each green strip. Retrace only the shapes shaded in gray, and cut them out using a craft knife. **(C)**

7 Choose one of the place mats from step 4, leaving it face down on your work surface. Using the glue stick, apply glue along all the edges of the cut out shapes.

8 Place a green strip onto the back of the glue-covered place mat and over the cut-outs (right side down), ½" (13mm) from the top and side of the place mat. Slightly

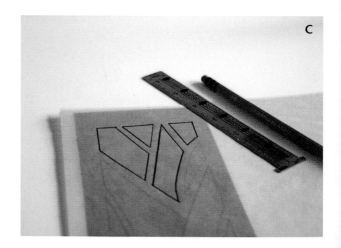

C

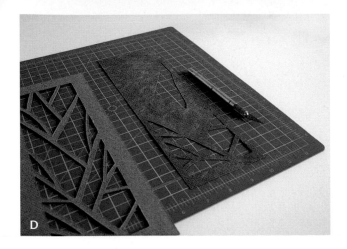

slide the green sheet ⅛" (3mm) down and ⅛" (3mm) towards the center of the place mat. Press firmly to adhere and remove any air bubbles. When the place mat is flipped over, the edges of the shapes that are cut out of the green paper will be slightly visible through the cutouts on the place mat. **(D)**

9 Repeat steps 7–8 with the remaining place mats and green strips.

To create a more durable, informal place mat, use lightweight paper for the background and the mat itself, then laminate it.

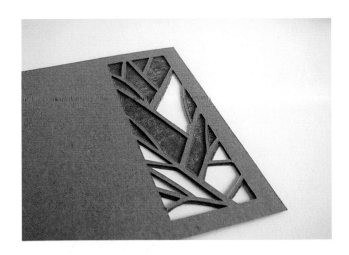

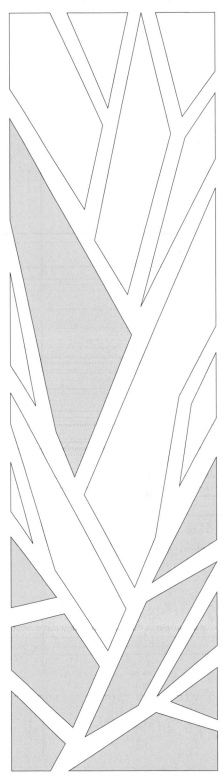

Pleated Table Runner

This is another project that uses simple materials and calls only for easy folding and cutting but appears sophisticated and intricate. Try using wrapping paper to create a runner with a variety of colors. The project easily adapts to fit a longer table or even to place mats. Just adjust the length of kraft paper and pleats to best fit your needs. See page 71 for coordinating napkin rings.

MATERIALS

3 strips of brown lightweight paper, 32" x 3" (81cm x 7.5cm), such as kraft paper

Bone folder

Ruler

Glue stick

Spray adhesive

1 sheet of brown lightweight paper, 53" x 12" (134.5cm x 30.5cm), such as kraft paper

2 strips of red heavy-weight paper, ⅜" x 12" (9mm x 30.5cm), such as card stock

FINISHED SIZE

53" x 12" (134.5cm x 30.5cm)

TIME: 1–2 HOURS . . . .

To reuse this project but adapt it for
a new celebration, replace the red strips
of paper with strips of a different color.

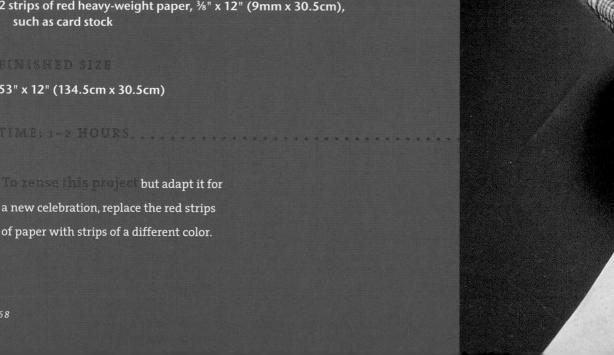

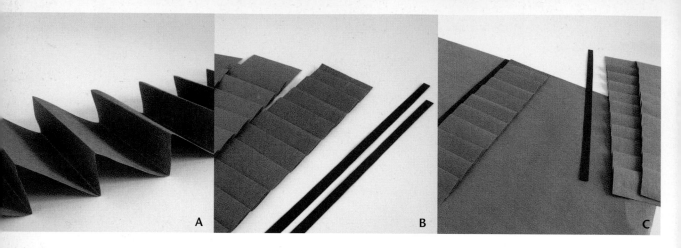

A

B

C

1 Starting 1½" (3.8cm) from the shortest end of a strip of brown kraft paper, score at alternating intervals of 1" (2.5cm) and 2" (5cm), making 9 sets of these folds. Add another scored line 1" (2.5cm) after the last scored line.

2 Fold the scored lines in pleated fashion. Start by folding the first 1" (2.5cm) interval under the following 2" (5cm) rectangle. Do the same for each pair of rectangles that follow. The 1" (2.5cm) intervals should not be visible from the outside. The 2" (5cm) rectangles will be folded over each of the 1" (2.5cm) intervals. **(A)**

3 Unfold the strip, and apply glue from the glue stick to the back side. Refold all the pleats, pressing them together to adhere.

4 Repeat steps 1–3 for the remaining 2 strips of brown kraft paper. **(B)**

5 To assemble the table runner, use spray adhesive to glue 1 pleated strip to the center of the large sheet of brown kraft paper (the runner). Glue the remaining 2 pleated strips 8" (20.5cm) from each short end of the runner. As you add each pleated strip, make sure that the openings of the pleats all face the same side of the runner. **(C)**

6 Using the glue stick, attach the red strips of card stock paper next to the inner sides of each of the two outer strips of pleated paper. **(D)**

tip*

If the runner gets a little dirty or

wrinkled, cut out and save the folded

strips and add them to a fresh sheet of

background paper.

D

Pleated Napkin Rings

Any table setting will look more welcoming simply by adding napkin rings. These rings not only look unique and stylish but also encourage recycling by using a paper towel roll as part of their construction. You can also cleverly revamp an old set of napkin rings you have around the house, or transform a plain pair from a discount store into a high-style home accessory. A set of napkins with your homemade pleated rings would make a lovely housewarming gift.

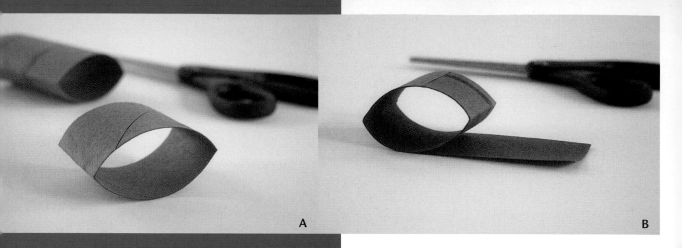

A   B

MATERIALS

1 empty paper towel roll or 4 smooth tube shaped napkin rings

Scissors

Ruler

Glue stick

4 strips of brown lightweight paper, 1½" x 5½" (3.8cm x 14cm), such as kraft paper

4 strips of red heavy-weight paper, ⅛" x 5½" (3mm x TKcm), such as card stock

4 strips of brown lightweight paper, ⅞" x 10" (2.2cm x 25.5cm), such as kraft paper

FINISHED SIZE

2¼" x 1½" (5.5cm x 3.8cm)

TIME: 1–2 HOURS

(to make 4 napkin rings)

1 Press a paper towel roll flat lengthwise and cut a 1½" (3.8cm) wide ring off one end. If using preexisting napkin rings, skip to step 2. **(A)**

2 Glue a 1½" x 5½" (3.8cm x 14cm) strip of brown kraft paper around the ring to completely cover the outer surface. Depending on the diameter of your ring, the ends of the strips may need to overlap slightly. **(B)**

3 Glue a red strip of card stock around and flush to one of the edges of the napkin ring. Make sure that the ends of the brown kraft paper and the red strip of card stock start and end on the same side of the ring (the back). **(C)**

tip*

- *Use a thin satin ribbon instead of the red*
- *paper strips for added contrast.*

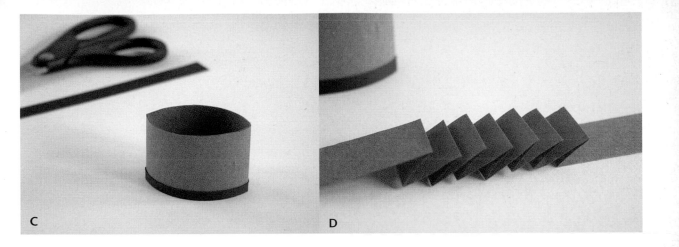

C

D

4 Score and fold a ⅞" x 10" (2.2cm x 25.5cm) strip of brown kraft paper along the short side, starting at the 2" (5cm) mark and continuing in alternating intervals of ½" (13mm) and ¾" (2cm), making 7 sets of these folds. The ½" (13mm) intervals should be tucked under the ¾" (2cm) intervals. All the pleats should be folded to the same side. **(D)**

5 Unfold the pleated strip, and apply glue to the back side of the entire strip. Refold the pleats, pressing them together to adhere.

6 Place the strip of 7 pleats centered on the ring and flush to the red strip of paper. The open end of the pleats should face the left. Glue the pleated strip into place, wrapping the ends around the back of the ring. The ends should overlap at the same place where the previous strips meet. **(E)**

7 Repeat steps 1–6 to make the remaining 3 napkin rings.

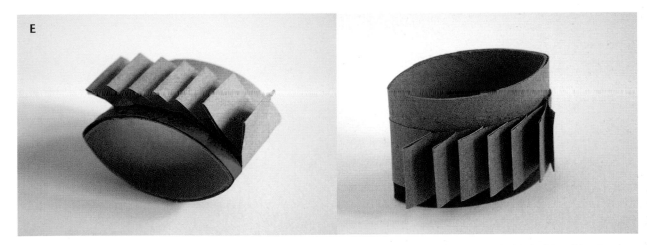

E

Globe Cupcake Toppers

This topper may be small but it makes a big visual statement. Make one to designate a special cupcake for a birthday boy or girl, or use several in a variety of colors on a group of cupcakes—just be sure to stock up on the materials you'll need. I love to coordinate this topper with the party decorations to create a festive, pulled-together atmosphere on the cheap. Use double-stick tape to string a bunch of these small globes on a decorative ribbon to create a brightly colored ceiling banner. Or make one or more large hanging globes using the design; just copy the template on page 77 at 200 percent and assemble. See page 77 for my favorite party decoration, using these small globes and the techniques from the Fluttering Mobile (page 16).

MATERIALS

1 sheet of tracing paper, 8½" x 11" (21.5cm x 28cm)

Soft pencil

Spray adhesive

6 sheets of white heavy-weight paper, 8½" x 11" (21.5cm x 28cm),
   such as card stock

6 sheets of orange heavy-weight paper, 8½" x 11" (21.5cm x 28cm),
   such as card stock

Scissors

Craft knife

Six 10" (25.5cm) wooden skewers

White PVA glue

Compass

FINISHED SIZE

2" x 2" x 6½" (5cm x 5cm x 16.5cm)

TIME: 1–2 HOURS

(to make 12 cupcake toppers)

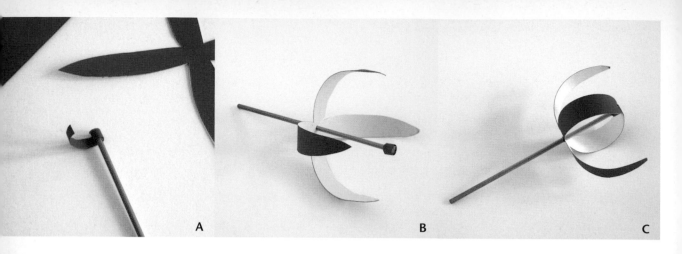

A   B   C

1 Copy the template on the facing page, and trace it onto the tracing paper with a soft pencil.

2 Using the spray adhesive, glue the white and orange card stock sheets together.

3 Place the tracing paper face down over a piece of white card stock, and retrace to transfer the image. Cut out the image along the outline.

4 Using the shape you have already cut out as a template, repeat step 3 with the remaining sheets of glued card stock, fitting two tracings on each sheet.

5 Using the craft knife, cut the wooden skewers so that they are 4¾" (12cm) long.

6 Cut 12 strips of orange card stock that are ⅛" x 4" (3mm x 10cm), and roll each around and flush to the top of a skewer. Dab a bit of white glue onto the end of each strip to seal the rolls. **(A)**

7 Poke a hole in the center of the card stock shapes using the sharp end of a compass.

8 Push a skewer through each hole with the white paper facing up. **(B)**

9 For each skewer, bend the 4 oval tips (without creasing them) toward the top of the skewer, and glue the inside tips of each to the top of the roll/skewer. Hold down the tips until dry. **(C), (D)**

D

- *Make several globes to top a cake, using*
- *different lengths of skewers to create an*
- *appealing grouping atop the frosting.*
- *To add a personal touch, write a special*
- *message inside the "petals" before closing*
- *each topper.*

Globe Topper Mobile

Though I love the simplicity of a single globe topper perched atop a cupcake, I often use the globe design as a springboard for other decorating ideas. In particular, I've found that substituting the globe shapes here for the folded circles in the Fluttering Mobile (page 16) produces a whimsical mobile reminiscent of childhood whirligigs and pinwheels. Because the finished globes are much bulkier than the delicate circles in the Fluttering Mobile project, you'll want to use a larger embroidery hoop to stabilize fewer strands of monofilament—and you can make far fewer globes to achieve a substantial effect. For my mobiles, I use a 10" (25.5cm) hoop and 6 strands of monofilament with 6–7 globes each separated by about 2" (5cm). Play around with the materials until you find a combination of globes, monofilament, and spacing that you like.

Box Flower String Lights

String lights are a great way to bring some mood lighting to your event.
These covers are deceptively quick and easy to make and can be customized according to the occasion and to complement any other decorations
for an event. White lights, as shown here, look great with colorful vellum
paper. If your string of lights is multicolored, white vellum would be ideal
for a polished look.

MATERIALS

3 sheets of fuchsia medium-weight paper, 8½" x 11" (21.5cm x 28cm),
   such as vellum paper

3 sheets of blue medium-weight paper, 8½" x 11" (21.5cm x 28cm),
   such as vellum paper

Ruler

Pencil

Scissors

Glue stick

String of lights with 50 lights

FINISHED SIZE

3" x 3" x 1½" (7.5cm x 7.5cm x 3.8cm)

TIME: 2–3 HOURS. . . . .

A   B   C

1 Measure and cut 25 strips each of fuchsia and blue vellum paper that are 1¼" x 5¼" (3cm x 13cm). **(A)**

2 Score each fuchsia strip parallel to the short side, 2" (5cm) from each end, and fold the 2 side edges toward each other. Unfold.

3 Attach 2 strips together by placing 1 perpendicularly on top of the other (forming a +) and gluing them together. The glue should be added to both the top of the center square of the bottom piece and the bottom of the square of the top piece. **(B)**

4 When the glue is dry, refold each of the 4 strip ends (or petals) toward the center. Curl each of the 4 petals outward by wrapping them around a pencil. Cut an X at the intersection of the 2 strips no wider than ¼" (6mm).

5 Repeat steps 2–4 using the blue vellum paper. **(C)**

6 Push the 50 light covers (alternating the fuchsia and blue covers) over the 50 lights on the strand. **(D)**

tip*

When selecting the cable lights, think about what kind of event you'll be illuminating. There are a multitude of cable and light bulb colors available. You can manipulate the look of the flowers to meet your needs, as well. For example, achieve a delicate style by trimming the flower tips in a rounded shape.

D

Leafy Centerpiece

This nature-inspired centerpiece brings the beauty of botanicals to any tabletop—and to those who cannot claim a green thumb. Unlike a real plant, this centerpiece requires no watering, making it a thoughtful hostess or housewarming gift. Change the colors of this arrangement to coordinate with any home decor, or match the colors for a particular event or the season of the year. Extra leaves can be cut out and used on napkin rings or as place cards for a formal dinner.

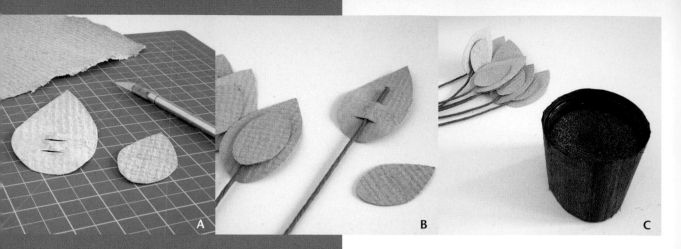

A   B   C

MATERIALS

1 sheet of tracing paper, 8½" x 11" (21.5cm x 28cm)

Soft pencil

1 sheet of cream textured medium-weight paper, 20" x 30" (51cm x 76cm), such as handmade paper

Craft knife

Cutting mat

Scissors

6 paper-wrapped stem wires, ⅛" x 18" (3mm x 45.5cm)

White PVA glue

1 sheet of dark brown medium-weight paper, 20" x 30" (51cm x 76cm), such as papyrus

Round glass container, 4" (10cm) in diameter and 3½" (9cm) tall

Sand

Glue stick

FINISHED SIZE

10" x 11" x 10" (25.5cm x 28cm x 25.5cm)

TIME: 2–3 HOURS

1 Copy the templates on the facing page. Trace each template on tracing paper with a soft pencil.

2 Place the tracing paper face down on the cream paper. Retrace each leaf another 11 times so that the pencil markings will transfer onto the cream paper. Make sure that you also retrace the 2 slits in the centers of the larger leaves.

3 Cut out all 24 leaves (12 large and 12 small). Using the craft knife, cut both slits in the center of each larger leaf. **(A)**

4 Using scissors, cut the paper-wrapped stem wires in half so that each is 9" (23cm) long.

5 Thread each paper-wrapped stem wire through 1 of the 12 large leaves. The stem wires must be inserted from the front of the leaf through the first slit and from the back toward the front of the leaf through the second slit.

6 On the area of each large leaf that is between the two slits, attach a small leaf using a dab of glue. **(B)**

7 Measure and cut the papyrus to 12" x 3½" (30.5cm x 9cm). Wrap the papyrus around the glass container, and seal the ends with the glue stick. Fill the container with sand. **(C)**

D

E

8 Bend the top third of each stem slightly outward. Form a circle that is about 1" (2.5cm) in diameter, and place 6 stems in the sand in the center of the container. The remaining 6 stems should be placed in the sand in a wider circle, with each stem between 2 stems of the first group. **(D), (E)**

Smaller leaves with shorter stem wires can be wrapped around wine glasses as wine charms.

tip *

* *If you want to imitate a real*
* *potted plant, use any clay or*
* *terra-cotta pot for the base of*
* *this project.*

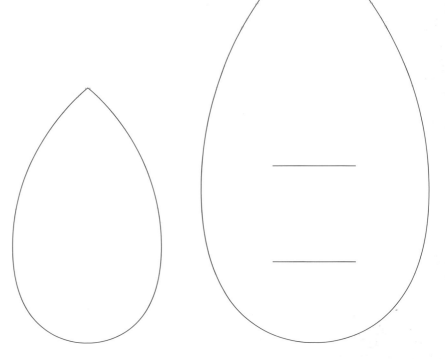

Fan Wine Charms

You can make your celebrations stylish with these playful—and practical—wine charms. I've always thought of them as an easy way to add color and a personal touch to a gathering. Not only is this project easy to make, but it also is a perfect opportunity to use assorted leftover scraps of colored paper.

MATERIALS

6 strips of white heavy-weight paper, 20" x ¼" (51cm x 6mm), such as card stock

6 strips of assorted heavy-weight paper, 15" x ¼" (38cm x 6mm), such as card stock

Push pin

Ruler

Craft knife

Cutting mat

1 wire hoop, 1" (2.5cm) diameter

60 small silver crimping beads

Pliers

FINISHED SIZE

2¾" x 2" x ¼" (7cm x 5cm x 6mm)

TIME: 1–2 HOURS

(to make 6 charms)

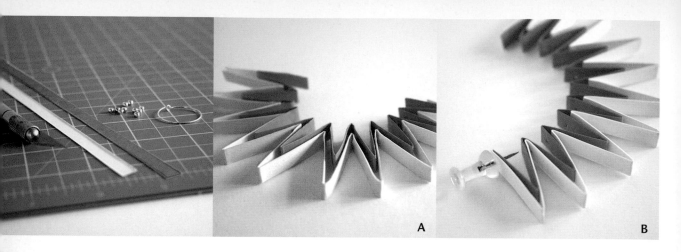

A

B

1 Crease and fold a strip of white card stock at 1" (2.5cm) intervals in accordion fashion.

2 Similarly, crease and fold a strip of the assorted card stock at ¾" (2cm) intervals in accordion fashion. In this example, I used a strip of turquoise card stock.

3 Keeping the strips creased, slide the folded tips of the turquoise strip into those of the white one. The inner folded ends of both strips should meet each other and be flush. This will be the side attached to the wire hoop. **(A)**

4 With a push pin, poke a hole through 1 end of the white and turquoise strips. The hole should be centered along the short end of the strips and ⅛" (3mm) from the end. **(B)**

5 Slide the strips onto the wire hoop. Slide on a crimp bead. Poke a second hole, centered along the width of the strip and ⅛" (3mm) from the fold, on the following fold of both strips. Slide the fold onto the wire hoop and add another bead.

tip*

I like the sophistication that the silver beads lend to these charms; however, I sometimes like to add more sparkle—especially at the holidays. To do so, just replace the silver crimp beads with glass beads. Of course, the colors of these beads can be coordinated, along with the paper colors, to match your party's theme.

C

The wine charms can be all made with the same two colors and personalized by writing each guest's name on one side of the charm. At the end of the event guests can take the charms home as small party favors.

· ·

6 Poke holes through the remaining folds and the opposite ends of the strips in same way as in steps 4–5, adding a bead in between each new fold. There is no need for a bead after the ends of the strips are added to the wire hoop. **(C)**

7 With a pair of pliers, twist the ⅛" (3mm) end of the straight end of the hoop into a hook (if yours doesn't have one). This hook will help secure the wire into the end loop of the hoop when the charm is placed on a wine glass. **(D)**

8 Repeat steps 1–7 to make the remaining 5 charms.

D

Contemporary Hurricane Candle Cover

Hurricane covers can turn your simple candles into striking table top statements. The professional look of these hurricane candles belies the simplicity of the project. Modern, elegant, and sophisticated, they require only materials handy in any office setting. Play around with the design of the negative space and see what kind of shadows your lights can cast. Rounded edged shapes will provide a softer appearance, for example.

I often cut out shapes that are similar to those on my tableware or linens, thus creating a special touch that can change as quickly as my tablecloth. My kids like to get in on the act at the holidays, cutting silhouettes of pine trees, snowflakes, and stars in the winter; simply decorated eggs in spring; and many kinds of leaves in the fall.

MATERIALS

2 sheets of lightweight paper, 8½" x 11" (21.5cm x 28cm), such as office paper

Ruler

Pencil

Scissors or craft knife

Glue stick

Glass hurricane candle, 4¾" (12cm) diameter x 9" (23cm) tall

FINISHED SIZE

4¾" x 9¼" (12cm x 23.5cm)

TIME: 30 MINUTES–1 HOUR. . . . .

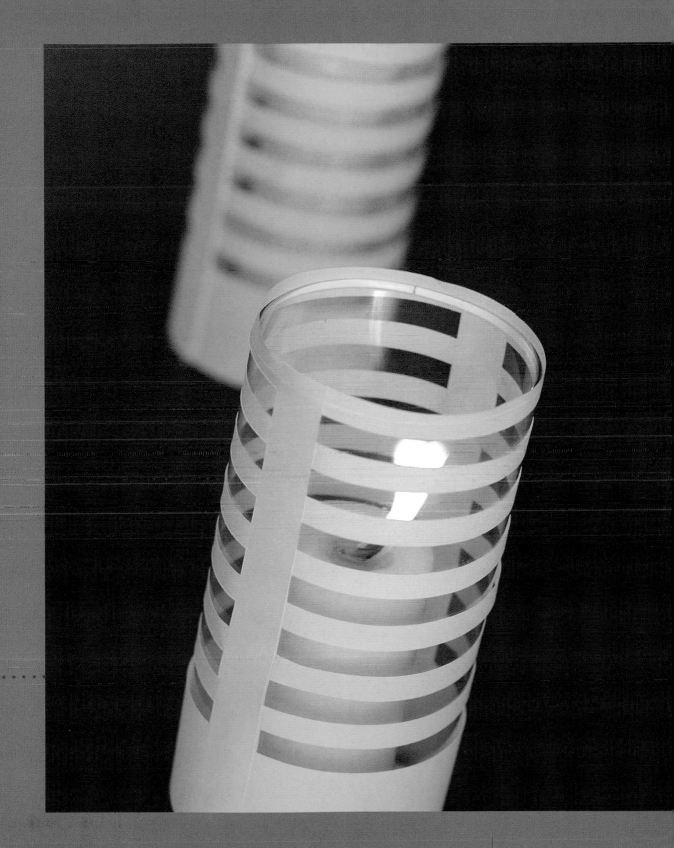

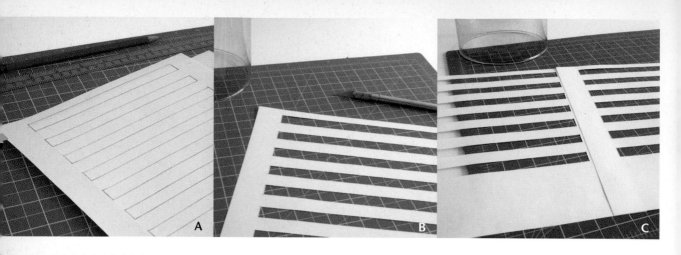

A

B

C

1 Cut each sheet of office paper to measure 8½" x 9¼" (21.5cm x 23.5cm).

2 Measure and draw seven 6½" x ½" (16.5cm x 13mm) rectangles centered on the first sheet, starting ½" (13mm) from the short end of the sheet and maintaining ½" (13mm) between each rectangle. **(A)**

3 Cut out all the rectangles with very sharp scissors or a craft knife and discard. **(B)**

4 Repeat steps 2–3 for the second page.

5 Glue 1 page to the other by overlapping 1 pair of the 1" (2.5cm) margins on the long side of each sheet. **(C)**

6 Create a cylinder by gluing the opposite side of the pages, overlapping the 1" (2.5cm) margins. Slide the cylinder over (and on the outside) of the glass hurricane candle. **(D)**

tip *

Vellum paper can be used for this project for a more translucent effect.

If you're making more than one hurricane candle cover, photocopy the design onto several sheets of paper so that duplication is quicker. Enlarge or shrink the design for hurricane candles of varying sizes. Decorating several glass hurricane candles with these covers will make a table top look stylish and enhance a candlelit event.

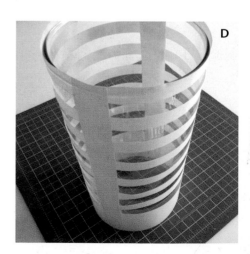

D

Most people do notice a gift's presentation. I know I do. The thought that goes into paper selection for a gift wrap or for a project that you've made yourself will let the person who is receiving it know they are special. It's always exciting to see how a person reacts when they open a gift. If you've carefully wrapped it, that happy feeling of satisfaction starts to set in before they even undo the package. Gifts made out of paper are very unique because they are so tactile and the work that is put in to them is so apparent. Your handiwork is something that a friend will surely appreciate.

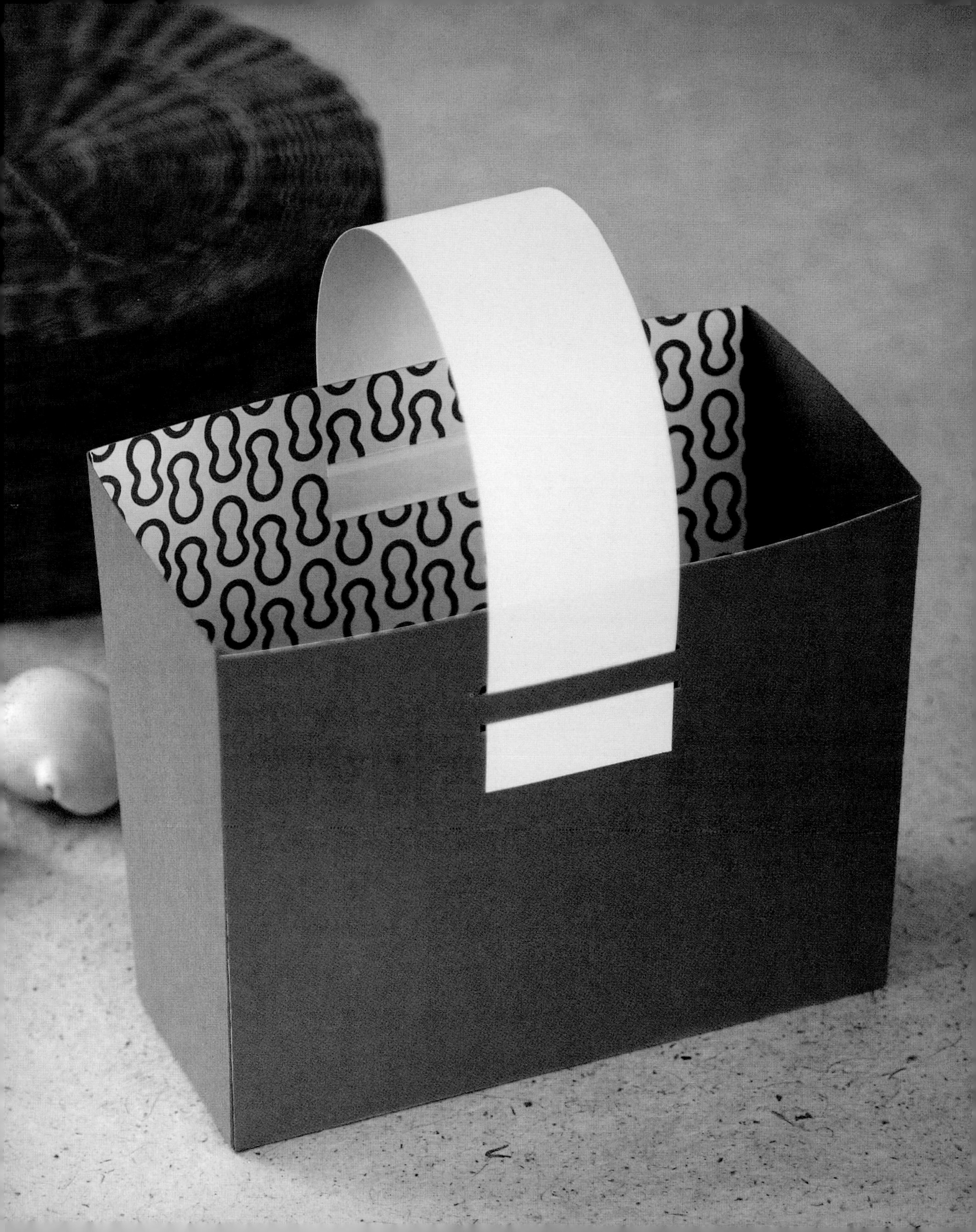

Gift Basket

Not every gift fits perfectly into a square box, and that's when I reach for this simple yet sophisticated gift basket. It's just the right size to hold gifts, party favors, or even a take-away snack. This basket is adaptable to any occasion, and its clean design allows your paper choice to really shine. And, your packaging will be sure to stand out in a crowd when made by hand.

It's also a great way to involve the whole family in wrapping a special gift, perhaps for the grandparents, a school friend, or a teacher. Once you've copied the template on the plain paper, have your kids add their artwork to it. Then, just cut, fold, and glue following the instructions. *Voila*! A personalized wrap that recipients can reuse around the house or for a future gift.

MATERIALS

1 sheet of tracing paper, 11" x 17" (28cm x 43cm)

Pencil

1 sheet of green heavy-weight paper, 18" (45.5cm) square, such as card stock

Scissors

Craft knife

Ruler

Bone folder

1 sheet of green patterned medium-weight paper, 18" (45.5cm) square, such as scrapbooking paper

Spray adhesive

1 sheet of white heavy-weight paper, 12" (30.5cm) square, such as card stock

FINISHED SIZE

7" x 8" x 4" (18cm x 20.5cm x 10cm)

TIME: 1–2 HOURS

Use chipboard in place of the card stock

to create a basket that will support items up to several pounds in weight.

1 Copy the template on the facing page at 223 percent. Trace the diagram of the basket with a soft pencil. Place the tracing paper face down on to the green card stock and retrace to transfer the drawing to the paper.

2 Score and fold all the straight edges. Keep the pencil markings on the inside of the basket. Cut out the 4 slits that were part of the transferred drawing. **(A)**

3 Measure and cut a 7" x 15" (18cm x 38cm) rectangle out of the green patterned paper. Use spray adhesive to glue it centered to the 3 rectangles of the same overall dimensions on the green card stock. **(B)**

4 Turn over the entire bag and, using a craft knife, remove the patterned paper from the 4 slits created in step 2. **(C)**

5 Add glue to the outer side of the 4 tabs that are adjacent to the area covered with the patterned paper. Press the tabs against the bottom and exposed side of the side flaps. **(D)**

6 To make the handle of the bag, cut a 12" x 2" (30.5cm x 5cm) rectangle out of the white card stock. Thread each short end of the handle into the bag from outside, through the top slit and out the bottom slit. Apply glue to the lower ¼" (6mm) of each short end of the handle, and attach them to the outside of the bag just below the lowest slit. **(E)**

tip*

For gifts that weigh more than a few pounds, create the handle from ribbon to add strength to the basket's construction—as well as contrasting texture to its presentation.

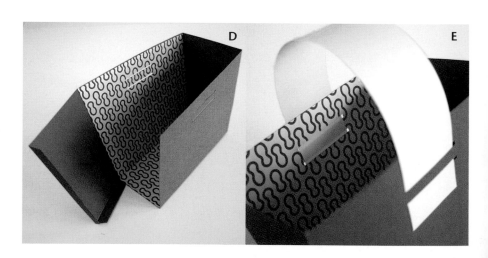

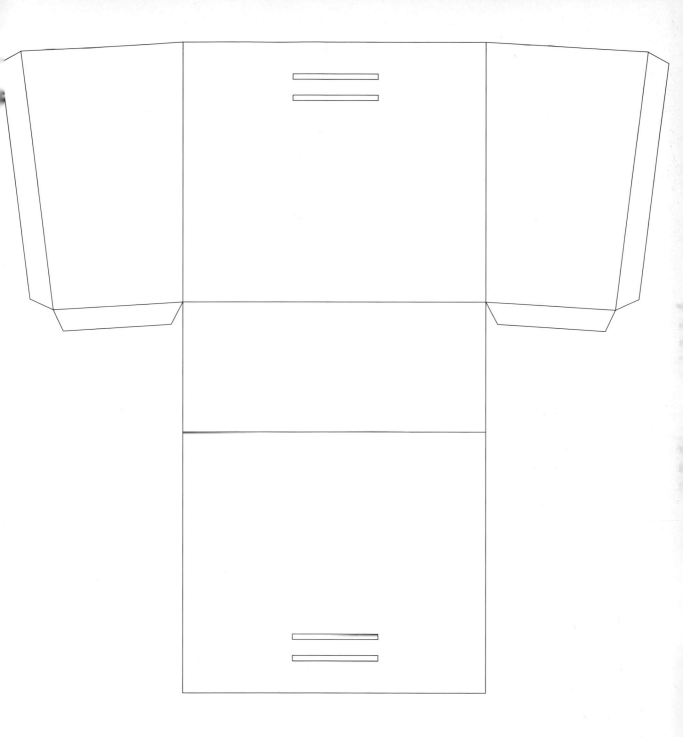

Magazine Bowl

I was inspired to design this project when I saw a set of square magazine coasters at a local store one day. Since I already own too many coasters, I decided to make a bowl instead. I used recycled magazine pages as my main material, but any type of paper of similar thickness can be used. Junk mail would be another suitable option, or even an old phone book—a wise choice for those who prefer a more subtle color palette.

One of the fun parts of this project is to choose paper randomly. Don't overthink your color choices and just use the sheets of paper that you've chosen in whatever order they present themselves.

MATERIALS:

60 to 80 sheets of medium-weight paper, such as pages torn out of a magazine

Scissors

Glue gun

Ruler

FINISHED SIZE

8½" x 3½" x 4" (21.5cm x 9cm x 10cm)

TIME: 3–4 HOURS . . . .

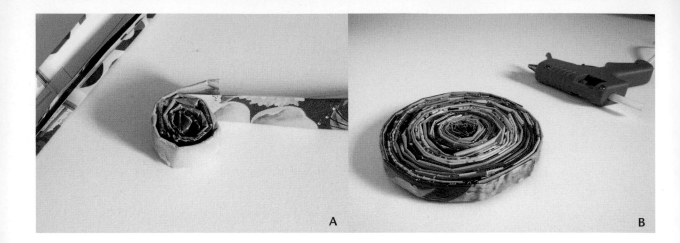

A

B

1 Cut each of the magazine pages in half lengthwise. Then, fold each page in half lengthwise about 3 times. The final width of each folded strip should be approximately ½" (13mm). It isn't necessary to fold them all before starting the project. You can fold them a few at a time, as you add them to the bowl.

2 Roll the first strip into a tight cylinder. As you roll the strip add a thin line of hot glue along the inside of the strip so that it doesn't fall apart. Only add a little bit of glue at a time because it dries fairly quickly. This first cylinder will form the bottom of the bowl.

3 Before the cylinder is completely closed, tuck a second strip under its edge. Make sure that both strips have the closed side of the folds on the same side of the cylinder. The side that has the closed folds will be the inside of the bowl. Continue adding a thin line of glue as you roll the second strip around the first and then around itself. **(A)**, **(B)**

Note Use as little glue as possible so that it doesn't seep out from under the edges. If it does, let it cool a bit (don't burn yourself!), and remove the excess glue. This will give your bowl a clean finish.

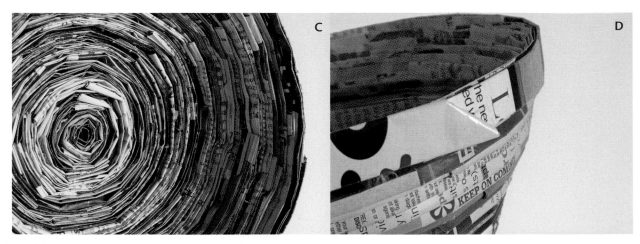

C

D

4 Continue to add to your cylinder, making sure that all the strips stay on the same level—your piece should be a flat disk. When your piece is about 5" (12.5cm) wide, glue the strips on each row that follows about ⅛" (3mm) higher than those in the previous row. **(C)**

5 Continue adding strips until your bowl is 4" (10cm) tall. Fold and glue the last ⅜" (9mm) of the visible ends of the strips on the last row diagonally. This will give your bowl a finished look. **(D)**

Just a Note Stationery Set and Folder

This stationery set is a thoughtful gift for someone who likes to keep in touch the old-fashioned way. You'll find instructions to make your own envelopes for this set (page 104), but if you are pressed for time, any A2-size envelopes will fit in this folder. Include a small set of stamps to make the set complete, and you may be getting a special message in the mail yourself.

MATERIALS

1 sheet of white heavy-weight paper, 18" square (45.5cm), such as card stock

Pencil

Ruler

Scissors

Bone folder

Glue stick

Five A2 blue envelopes, 4⅜" x 5¾" (11cm x 14.5cm) (page 104)

Five A2 orange envelopes, 4⅜" x 5¾" (11cm x 14.5cm) (page 104)

10 sheets of blue medium-weight paper, 5½" x 8½" (14cm x 21.5cm), such as stationery paper

10 sheets of orange medium-weight paper, 5½" x 8½" (14cm x 21.5cm), such as stationery paper

1 strip of blue patterned medium-weight paper, 14" x 2.5" (35.5cm x 6.5cm), such as scrapbooking paper

1 strip of orange medium-weight paper, 14" x 3" (35.5cm x 7.5cm), such as scrapbooking paper

1 white ribbon, 15" x ⅛" (38cm x 3mm)

FINISHED SIZE

6" x 9½" x ¼" (15cm x 24cm x 6mm)

TIME: 2–3 HOURS.

1 To create the body of the folder, measure and cut an 18" x 10½" (45.5cm x 26.5cm) rectangle out of the white card stock.

2 Draw a line ½" (13mm) from each long edge of the rectangle. Make a hash mark on each line 3" (7.5 cm) from one end.

3 Use a ruler and craft knife to slice the paper straight from the hash marks out to the paper's edges, separating each ½" (13mm) margin on the card stock into 1 long and 1 short rectangle. Then, cut away the long rectangles along the lines drawn in step 2.

4 Cut the exposed corners of the 2 small rectangles on the diagonal to create tabs (Papercraft Secret, page 43). Score and fold them toward the center of the card stock. **(A)**

5 Measure, score, and crease vertical lines parallel to the short end of the card stock at the following points, measuring from the left side of the paper for each crease: 2½" (6.5cm), 2¾" (7cm), 8¾" (22cm), 9" (23cm), and 15" (38cm). These creases will form 6 rectangles along the page, left to right. **(B)**

6 Fold the rectangle with tabs above and below it inward, toward the left panel. Add glue to the underside of the

tabs, and press them against the inside of the back of the folder (the second rectangle from right to left). You have now created the main pocket for the stationery.

7 To create the envelope pockets, cut two 5¾" x 5½" (14.5cm x 14cm) rectangles out of the remaining white card stock.

8 Choose 1 of these rectangles. First, draw a 4¾" x 5⅛" (12cm x 14cm) rectangle that is centered on and flush to the longest side (the top). Then, draw a 5" x 5" (14cm x 14cm) square that is also centered on and flush to the longest side. These two outlines will overlap one another and form two vertical rectangles and one horizontal rectangle. **(C)**

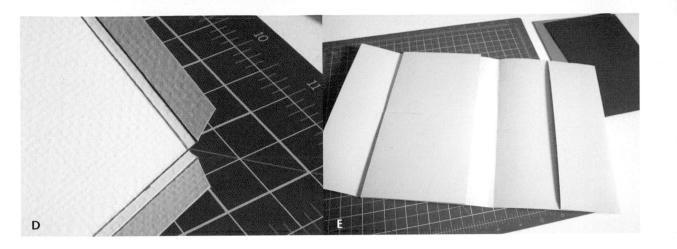

D

E

9 Extend the intersection of these rectangles outward to the edges of the paper, forming two 1" (13mm) squares. Cut out these squares. Then score and fold along the lines drawn in step 8 to create the sides of the pocket and the tabs. Diagonally trim the outer corners of each tab. **(D)**

10 Repeat steps 7–9 to make the other pocket with the second piece of card stock cut out in step 7.

11 To finish assembling the folder, apply glue to the backs of the pocket tabs. Glue the tabs down by aligning the pockets so that their closed ends are flush to the fold created in step 4 at 2¾" (7cm). **(E)**

12 Once the glue has dried, slide the sheets of stationery into the large pocket and 5 envelopes into each of the smaller pockets. **(F)**

13 To create the sash, apply glue to the underside of the blue patterned paper. Center it atop the orange paper and press to seal. Close the stationery folder and wrap the sash horizontally around it so that the ends of the sash overlap at the back of the folder. Using a glue stick, glue these overlapped areas together. The sash should fit snugly but still comfortably slide on and off the folder. Tie the ribbon around the sash, forming a knot or a bow at the center of the front of the sash. If desired, dab a small amount of glue between the ribbon and the sash to secure. **(G)**

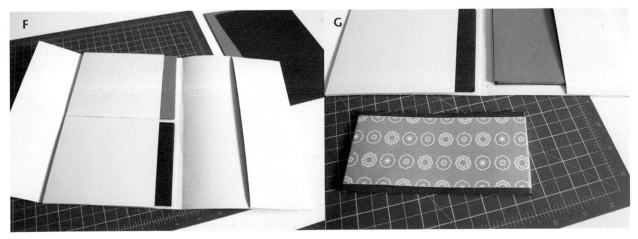

F

G

A2-size envelopes

Handmade envelopes are quick and easy to create—and make any handwritten note extra special. Follow these simple steps to make custom envelopes that will fit perfectly in the Just a Note Stationery Folder.

1 Draw a 4⅜" x 5¾" (11cm x 14.5cm) rectangle in the center of a medium-weight sheet of paper that measures 10¾" x 10½" (27cm x 26.5cm). This side of the sheet will be the inside of your envelope.

2 With a ruler, find the center of one of the long sides of the rectangle. Make a small pencil mark at that point.

3 Turn your ruler perpendicular to the edge of the rectangle and aligned on the pencil mark. Make a second mark on the edge of the sheet closest to the first mark.

4 Draw a line from the second mark to each of the nearest corners of the rectangle. This triangle will be the envelope flap.

5 Repeat steps 2–4 for each of the remaining three sides.

7 Cut along the outer edge of all four triangles.

8 Cut 1" (2.5cm) off the tip of the triangle opposite from the flap of the envelope. The cut must be made perpendicular to the bottom long edge of the rectangle.

9 Score and fold all four sides of the triangle. Erase all pencil marks.

10 Fold in the triangles on the left and right of the rectangle.

11 Fold the bottom shape over the left and right triangles. Use a glue stick to glue only the sections of paper that overlap one another.

Chic Gift Bag

I designed this bag to hold those small gifts that are difficult to wrap with paper. This bag can even be used for storing small items. The look will drastically change according to the paper and ribbon you use. Once you've mastered making this bag, try creating some of different sizes—a long, thin bag would be perfect for a bottle of wine.

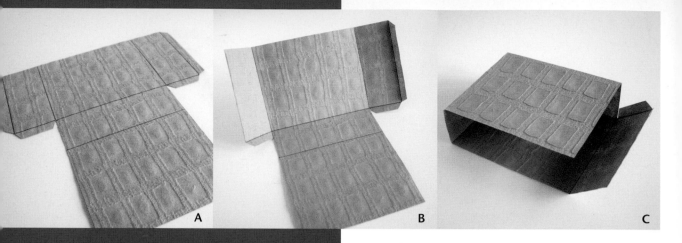

A   B   C

MATERIALS

1 sheet of textured medium-weight paper, 20" x 30" (51cm x 76cm), such as handmade embossed paper

Pencil

Ruler

Scissors

Glue stick

Round hole punch, ½" (13mm) diameter

Ribbon, ¼" x 12" (6mm x 30.5cm)

FINISHED SIZE

6" x 2" x 5" (15cm x 5cm x 12.5cm)

TIME: 30 MINUTES—1 HOUR

1 Measure and draw a 6" x 2" (15cm x 5cm) rectangle on the back of the sheet of textured paper. The top left corner of the rectangle should be 6" (15cm) from the top and 5" (12.5cm) from the left side of the sheet.

2 Measure and draw 2 additional rectangles, each measuring 6" x 5" (15cm x 12.5cm), 1 above and 1 below the first rectangle. The rectangles should be adjacent to and each share a long side with the rectangle made in step 1.

3 Measure and draw 2 more rectangles, each measuring 2" x 5" (5cm x 12.5cm), 1 to the right and 1 to the left of the rectangle drawn in step 1. These rectangles should each share a short side to the rectangle from step 1.

4 Measure and draw 4 rectangles, 2 each measuring ½" x 5" (5cm x 12.5cm) adjacent to the long, outer edges of the rectangles made in step 3, and 2 each measuring 2" x ½" (5cm x 12.5cm) adjacent to the short, bottom edges of the rectangles drawn in step 3.

5 Cut out the complete shape, and then cut through the ½" (13mm) end of the rectangles drawn in step 4 that keep them attached to the main piece. Then cut the 2 exposed corners of each of these rectangles on a diagonal to turn them into tabs (Papercraft Secret, page 43). **(A)**

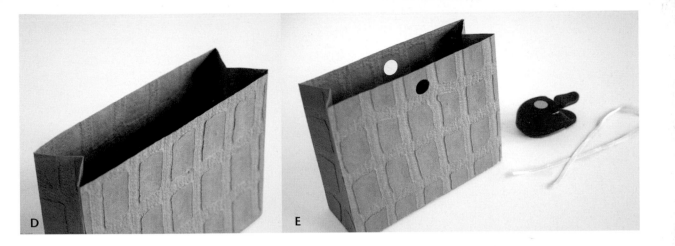

6 Score and fold where all the lines are drawn. The pencil markings should all be left on the inside of the bag. If some pencil markings are very noticeable, erase them (only *after you've scored and folded!*). **(B)**

7 Press and hold together the outermost corners (right sides facing each other) of the short ends of the rectangles made in step 3, and crease about 2" (5cm) down the centerline along the length of the rectangle.

8 Add glue to the outer side of the 4 tabs made in steps 4 and 5, and attach them to the inside of the larger rectangles made in step 2. **(C)**, **(D)**

9 Punch a hole through the front and back panels of the bag, centered ½" (13mm) from the top edge. **(E)**

10 Close the bag by lacing the ribbon through the holes and tying it in a bow.

tip *

- If this bag is made using a solid colored sheet of paper,
- you can easily decorate it with rubber stamps, your own
- doodles, stickers, or anything else you can think of. The
- design is simple enough that it won't seem overdone. I
- like to decorate mine with the flower used for the Flower
- Favor Box on page 128.

Fresh-Picked Recipe Box and Dividers

A recipe box is a useful housewarming or bridal shower gift, especially if some special family recipes are included. The modern cutout branch design provides a subtle touch of color and decor without overwhelming the surface of the box. The colors of this recipe box happen to match my own kitchen, but they can be easily changed to suit your taste.

MATERIALS

1 sheet of 2-ply heavy-weight paper, 15½" x 18½" (39.5cm x 46cm), such as chipboard

Ruler

Pencil

Cutting knife

Cutting mat

Eraser

White PVA glue

1 sheet of tracing paper, 8½" x 11" (21.5cm x 28cm)

3 sheets of mustard yellow heavy-weight paper, 12" (30.5cm) square, such as card stock

1 sheet of white lightweight paper, 8½" x 11" (21.5cm x 28cm), such as office paper

Scissors

FINISHED SIZE

6½" x 4½" x 4" (16.5cm x 11.5cm x 10cm)

TIME: 2–3 HOURS . . . .

A   B   C

1 Measure and draw a 6½" x 3" (16.5cm x 7.5cm) rectangle centered on the short side of the chipboard. This will be the front top half of the box.

2 Draw a rectangle adjacent and just below the one drawn in step 1 that is the same width and 4" (10cm) tall. This will be the top of the box.

3 Draw a 6½" x 4½" (16.5cm x 11.5cm) rectangle adjacent to the rectangle drawn in step 2. This will be the back of the box.

4 Draw a rectangle, below the one drawn in step 3, that is 6½" x 4" (16.5cm x 10cm). This will be the bottom of the box. Then draw two 4½" x 4" (11.5cm x 10cm) rectangles, one on each side of it. These will be the sides of the box.

5 Draw two 4½" x ½" (11.5cm x 13mm) rectangles adjacent to and above each of the 2 rectangles drawn last in step 4. Using a craft knife, cut the ½" (13mm) vertical slit that attaches each of them to the rectangle between them. Cut the outer corners of these rectangles on a diagonal (Papercraft Secret, page 43).

6 Draw a 6½" x 3" (16.5cm x 7.5cm) rectangle below the first rectangle drawn in step 4. This is the front bottom half of the box.

7 Draw two 3" x ½" (7.5cm x 13mm) rectangles below the last rectangles drawn in step 4 and adjacent to the rectangle between them (from step 6). Cut the ½" (13mm) vertical slit that attaches each of them to the rectangle between them. Cut the outer corners of these rectangles on a diagonal.

8 Cut around the entire outline of the box, using the cutting knife and mat. Score and fold all the straight edges of the rectangles, keeping the pencil markings on the inside. Gently erase the pencil markings. **(A)**

9 Apply glue to the outer rectangle tabs created in steps 5 and 7, and glue them to the inside of the rectangles that are adjacent to each of the smaller rectangles when the box is folded up.

10 Copy the branch template on the facing page and trace with a soft pencil onto tracing paper. Turn the tracing paper face down on to the yellow card stock, and retrace 2 times so that the pencil drawing will transfer. Cut out the 2 branch drawings with scissors.

11 Cut 4 ovals out of white paper, large enough to cover the center of the 2 top leaves of each branch. Add glue to the perimeter of the ovals, and attach them to the back of each of the 4 top leaves.

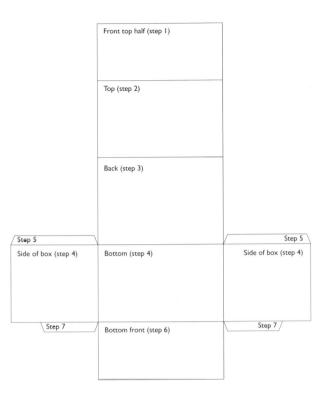

Front top half (step 1)

Top (step 2)

Back (step 3)

Step 5   Step 5

Side of box (step 4)   Bottom (step 4)   Side of box (step 4)

Step 7   Step 7

Bottom front (step 6)

12 Cut the first drawing across, making the lower part of the branch 3" (7.5cm) tall. Set the top part of the branch aside. Glue the lower part of the branch to the front of the recipe box. Place it flush to the bottom of the box and ½" (13mm) from the right edge.

13 Close the box (the flap will tuck inside the front rectangle) and glue the upper part of the branch on the top cover and flap so that it forms a complete branch design. **(B)**

14 Glue the second, uncut branch to the inside back panel of the recipe box. Place it 2½" (6.5cm) from the bottom and ½" (13mm) from the left edge. **(C)**

tip*

- *Cut out an extra leafy branch and use it*
- *as a template to draw the outline of the*
- *illustration onto each of the dividers.*

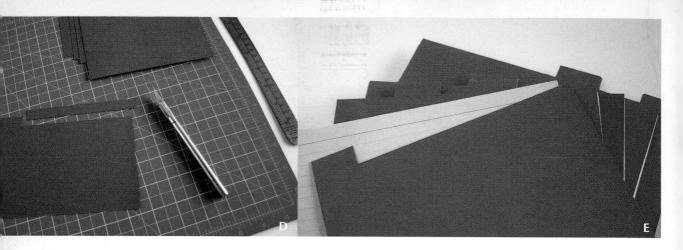

15 Cut out 6 rectangles that are 6" x 4⅜" (15cm x 11.1cm) from the mustard card stock. Draw a line along the longer side of the each card that is ½" (13mm) from the top edge. These will become the recipe card dividers.

16 On 1 card, draw a ½" (13mm) vertical line 1" (2.5cm) from the top left edge. Cut out the rectangle that is to the right of the ½" (13mm) line. This will create a tab for your divider. **(D)**

17 For the second divider, draw two ½" (13mm) vertical lines from the top of the second card at 1" (2.5cm) and 2" (5cm) from the left edge, respectively. Cut out the rectangles on the left and the right sides of the newly drawn tab.

18 For the third divider, draw two ½" (13mm) vertical lines from the top of a card at 2" (5cm) and 3" (7.5cm) from the left edge. Cut out the rectangles on the left and the right sides of the newly drawn tab.

19 Repeat step 16 for the fourth card and step 17 for the fifth card. Flip these 2 cards over so the tabs are on the right sides of the cards. **(E)**

20 A new set of divider cards can be created as needed. Use standard 4" x 6" (10cm x 15cm) note cards between the dividers to write the recipes on.

An easy way to save time but retain this project's handcrafted appeal would be to purchase a plain wooden recipe box and glue a set of the cutout leafy branches to it.

Double-Bow Gift Topper

This gift topper is the whimsical solution for a package that needs an extra special touch. Pick card stock that will complement your wrapping paper, and you'll bestow an unforgettable gift. Decorating boxes isn't the only use for this project. Smaller versions of this gift topper can be used as tree ornaments, to decorate the tops of napkin rings, or to attach to gift bags.

A

B

C

MATERIALS

1 sheet of tracing paper, 8½" x 11" (21.5cm x 28cm)

Pencil

1 sheet of green heavy-weight paper, 12" (30.5cm) square, such as card stock

Scissors

Glue stick

1 sheet of white heavy-weight paper, 8½" x 11" (21.5cm x 28cm), such as card stock

Hole punch, ½" (13mm) diameter

FINISHED SIZE

4" x 1½" x 4" (10cm x 3.8cm x 10cm)

TIME: 30 MINUTES–1 HOUR

Instead of using one sheet of card stock, glue 2 medium-weight papers back to back to make a multicolored or multipatterned topper.

1 Copy the template on the facing page at 200 percent and trace it with a soft pencil. Place the tracing paper face down on the green card stock paper, and retrace the template onto the paper twice.

2 Cut out the 2 shapes along the outline of the transferred drawing. **(A)**

3 Lay one cutout across the other, lining up the circular shapes in the center, to form a + shape. Attach both cutouts using the glue stick in the center of the small circles, where both pieces overlap.

4 Cut 2 strips out of the white card stock that measure ½" x 4" (13mm x 10cm) and ¼" x 4" (6mm x 10cm).

D

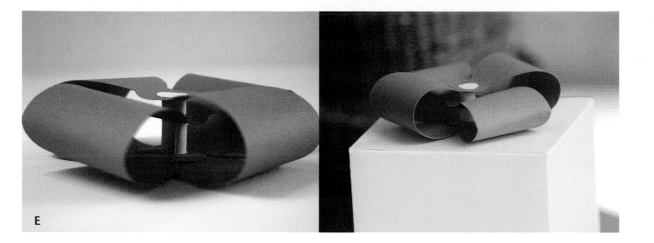

E

5 Tightly roll each strip around a pencil, and seal the end with glue. Slide the rolls of paper off the pencil.

6 Your rolls may not be exactly the same size. Choose the widest roll, and glue it over the spot where the 2 green card stock shapes (or petals) overlap. **(B)**

7 Take the 2 ends of the green card stock petals that are directly beneath the roll, and bring them over the roll of white card stock (leave the remaining 2 petals alone for now). Glue them to one another and to the top of the roll as well. Make sure that the circular ends of each strip line up one over the other. **(C)**, **(D)**

8 Glue the base of the second roll of white card stock above the 2 folded-over petals, aligning this roll with the one below the petals.

9 Take the ends of the remaining green card stock petals, the ones on the very bottom of the topper, and bring them over the second roll of white card stock. Glue them to one another and to the top of the roll as well. Make sure that the circular ends of each strip line up one over the other. **(E)**

10 Using the hole punch, punch out a circle from white card stock. Glue the circle in the top middle of the bow.

tip*

Create this gift topper to top a present from your kitchen. It's easy to picture this pretty paper bow atop a gift-themed cake.

Pocket Photo Album

A photo album is a wonderful gift for family members or friends. Now that digital cameras have taken over the photography market, so many of us only view our photos online or on our computers. This album will keep memories within arm's reach and can be customized to suit a specific event or personal tastes.

MATERIALS

1 sheet of dark gray heavy-weight paper, 20" x 30" (51cm x 76cm), such as acid-free Canson paper

Ruler

Pencil

Bone folder

Eraser

Glue stick

Hole punch

1 sheet of patterned medium-weight paper, 12" (30.5cm) square, such as acid-free scrapbooking paper

5 sheets of white medium-weight paper, 8½" x 11" (21.5cm x 28cm), such as acid-free card stock

1 ribbon, ½" x 14" (13mm x 35.5cm)

1 box of archival-quality photo mounting corners

FINISHED SIZE

8½" x 5½" x ¼" (21.5cm x 14cm x 6mm)

TIME: 2–3 HOURS . . . .

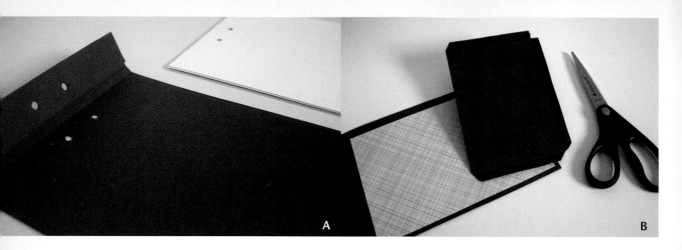

A

B

1 Measure and cut a rectangle that is 19" x 5½" (48.5cm x 14cm) from the Canson paper.

2 Mark and draw lines parallel to the short end of the rectangle at the 1" (2.5cm), 2" (5cm), 2¼" (5.5cm), 10¾" (27.3cm), and 11" (28cm) points. With the bone folder, score and crease each one.

3 Fold over and glue the first 1" (2.5cm) rectangle over the rectangle adjacent to it.

4 Fold the glued rectangles from step 3 over the album, keeping the spine straight.

Note You have now created a 1" (2.5cm) front flap closure and a ¼" (6mm) spine. As you work, do not allow the spine to fold at an angle. Extra folding will result in a worn edge at the fold. If keeping the spine straight before binding proves difficult, place a ¼" (6mm) stack of scrap paper between the back cover and the front flap closure.

5 Cut a ½" x 5½" (13mm x 14cm) rectangle out of the patterned paper. Glue it centered along the front flap closure.

6 Punch 2 holes in the center of the front flap closure that are 1" (2.5cm) apart and ½" (13mm) from the edge of the album. The holes should go through the glued rectangles and through to the back of the album. **(A)**

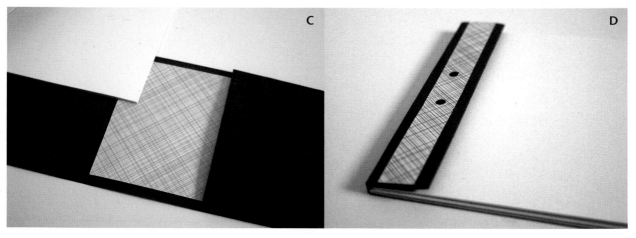

C

D

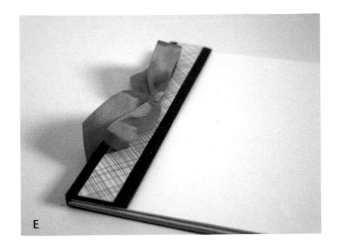

E

tip*
: *If photographs will be placed on facing*
: *pages, protect them by inserting a sheet*
: *of tissue paper between each page.*

7 Cut a 7½" x 5" (19cm x 12.5cm) rectangle out of the patterned paper. Center and glue it to the inside front cover of the album. The front cover is the larger rectangle on the opposite end of the rectangles from step 3.

8 To make the inside pocket, cut out a 4½" x 6½" (11.5cm x 16.5cm) rectangle out of the gray Canson paper. Measure tabs that are ½" (13mm) wide on the top, bottom, and 1 side of the rectangle. Cut out two ½" (13mm) squares out of the corners that are between the 3 tabs. Fold and crease each pocket tab. **(B)**

9 Using the glue stick, apply glue to the outer part of each tab. Turn the pocket over, and glue it to the inside of the album front cover. The pocket should be flush to the 3 outermost edges of the cover. **(C)**

10 Cut the 5 white card stock sheets in half crosswise, making ten 5½" x 8½" (14cm x 21.5cm) sheets.

11 Punch 2 holes into each of the 10 white card stock sheets that are centered on the short end of the cards, ½" (13mm) from the short end of the cards, and 1" (2.5cm) apart.

12 Slide the white card stock sheets into the album. Line up all the holes from the back cover, white sheets, and front tab. Thread the ribbon through the holes, and make a bow on the front of the album. **(D)**, **(E)**

13 Use 4 archival-quality mounting corners to attach each photo to the pages of the album. Extra photos can be placed in the pocket.

14 To close the album, slide the front cover under the front flap (like a match book).

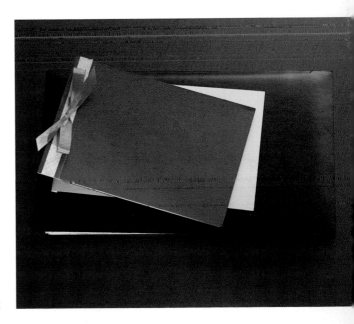

Monogrammed Journals Set

This set of month-by-month journals would make a great gift for someone who likes to write down their thoughts or enjoys having a sketchbook handy. It would also make a thoughtful gift for a busy new mom—the journals are just the right size to keep on hand to preserve precious moments, funny anecdotes, pictures, clippings, and other notes about baby. The covers of this particular set have the letters of the months on them, and I've included templates for each. But I've given these to others with their first initials on the covers, as well as with simple silhouettes like animals. Just trace or draw the shape you want to use at step 5, and then continue making journals following the instructions.

MATERIALS

12 sheets of taupe heavy-weight paper, 8½" x 11" (21.5cm x 28cm), such as card stock

120 sheets of white lightweight paper, 8½" x 11" (21.5cm x 28cm), such as office paper

Binder's needle

Binder's thread

Ruler

1 sheet of tracing paper, 8½" x 11" (21.5cm x 28cm)

Pencil

Cutting mat

Craft knife

12 sheets of assorted patterned medium-weight papers, 3" (7.5cm) square, such as scrapbooking paper

Glue stick

1 sheet of brown heavy-weight paper, at least 13" x 8⅝" (33cm x 22cm), such as corrugated cardboard

Bone folder

White PVA glue

FINISHED SIZE

5½" x 8⅝" x 2" (14cm x 22cm x 5cm)

TIME: 3–4 HOURS. . . . .

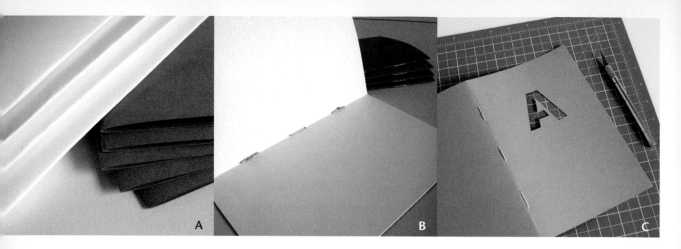

A   B   C

1 Fold all the taupe and white paper in half. The folded size should be 5½" x 8½" (14cm x 21.5cm). Divide and slide the white sheets inside one another in 12 groups of 10 sheets each. Slide each of these stacks into 1 of the taupe sheets. All the spines of the white and taupe sheets should be on the same side. **(A)**

2 Open up one of the books and, using the needle, poke 3 pairs of holes along the spine, each pair with 1" (2.5cm) between the 2 holes. One pair of holes should be in the center of the spine and the other 2 pairs should be 1½" (3.8cm) away from either edge of the book, which will leave 1¼" (3cm) between the pairs of holes.

3 Use 1 of the pages from the first book as a guide for the rest of the books. Place the page in the center of each of the other 11 books and mark all 6 points with a pencil. Pierce all the marked spots with a needle.

4 Starting from the center spread of each book, sew all of the pages together (including the taupe cover) by going around and into each set of holes twice. Tie the 2 loose ends of the thread used for each pair of holes on the inside of the book. **(B)**

5 Copy the letters on the facing page at 200 percent, and trace them onto tracing paper. Using a soft pencil, redraw the letters corresponding to the first letter of each month

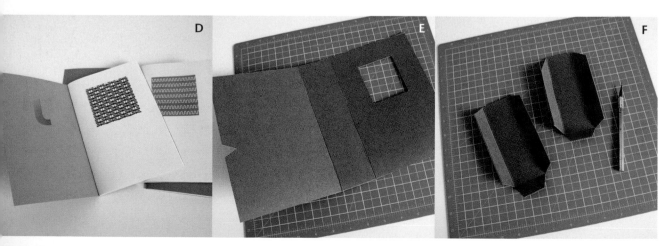

D   E   F

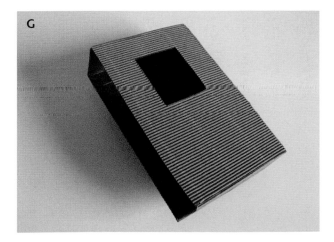

tip*

- To save time, staple the pages of these journals
- together instead of sewing. Then disguise the staples
- by covering each spine with a 2" x 8½" (5cm x 21.5cm)
- strip of paper.

in the center and 1¾" (4.5cm) from the top of each cover. Open the book and place just the front cover onto a cutting mat, then cut out each letter with a craft knife. **(C)**

6 Using the glue stick, glue 1 of the 12 assorted colored squares of paper to the first inside page of each journal. Each square should be centered on the page and 1" (2.5cm) from the top so the color will show through the cutout letter on the cover. **(D)**

7 To make the box for the journals, cut a 13" x 8⅝" (33cm x 22cm) rectangle out of the corrugated cardboard.

8 Score and fold the cardboard at 5½" (14cm) and 7½" (19cm) from the short end of the rectangle.

9 With the outside of the cover face down, measure and cut out a 2½" x 3" (6.5cm x 7.5cm) rectangle that is centered on the right-hand side of the cover and 1¼" (3cm) from the top.

10 Measure and cut out a small triangle shape on the long open side of the left or back cover of the box. Center the triangle's 1" (2.5cm) wide base on the box cover edge and make the triangle 1½" (3.8cm) tall. **(E)**

11 To make the top and bottom of the box, cut two 3½" x 5½" (9cm x 14cm) rectangles out of the remaining corrugated cardboard. To create tabs, score and fold twice, ¾" (2cm) away from each long side. Cut the outer corners of these tabs on a diagonal (Papercraft Secret, page 43). **(F)**

12 Apply glue to the outer part of the tabs, then attach the top and bottom sections of the box using white glue. **(G)**

13 When all the glue is dry, slide the journals into the box with their spines facing outward. The letter of the month of the first journal should be visible through the window on the box cover.

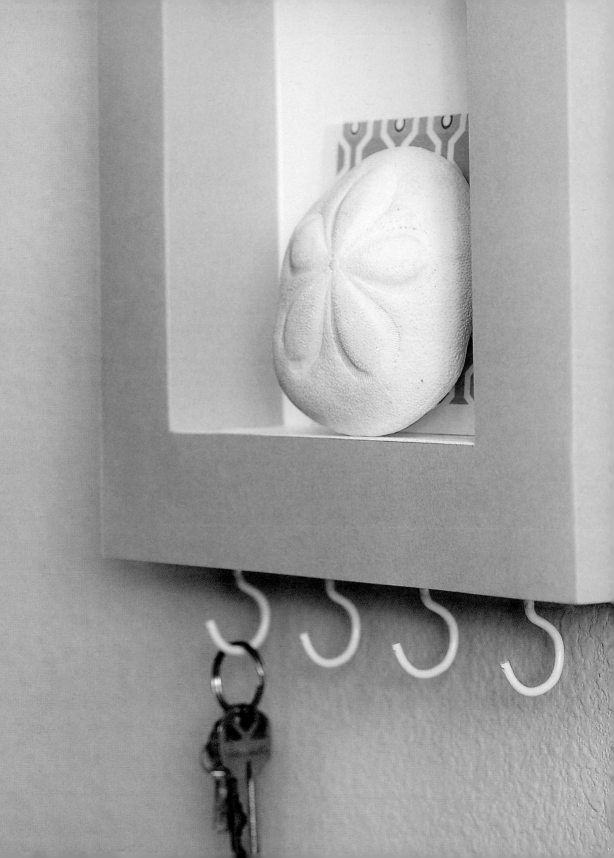

Hooked-Up Key Holder

This key holder is a convenient project to hang close to an entryway. Since I made mine, we haven't lost a set of keys yet! The inset square acts like the Light as Air Floating Cubby (page 40) and can be used to display small objects. Make one for each member of the family.

MATERIALS

1 piece of thick cardboard, 10" (25.5cm) square

1 wooden block, 10" x 1¾" x 1¾" (25.5cm x 4.5cm x 4.5cm)

White PVA glue

Drill and drill bit (suitable for the width of the hooks)

4 white metal screw hooks

1 sheet of tracing paper, 11" x 17" (28cm x 43cm)

Pencil

1 sheet of white heavy-weight paper, 12" (30.5cm), such as card stock

Bone folder and ruler

1 sheet of blue heavy-weight paper, 18" (45.5cm), such as card stock

Glue stick

Scissors

FINISHED SIZE

10" x 11¾" x 1¾" (25.5cm x 27cm x 4.5cm)

TIME: 2–3 HOURS

A B C

1 Using a pencil, poke a hole centered and 1" (2.5cm) from an edge of the sheet of cardboard. This is the hole from which the key holder will be hung.

2 Using white PVA glue, adhere the wooden block flush along the opposite edge of the cardboard. This is the only step that will use the PVA glue. Use the glue stick for the remainder of the steps. **(A)**

3 Drill 4 holes that are 2" (5cm) apart from one another, centered along the width of the wooden block and at least ½" (13mm) deep. Screw in the 4 hooks.

4 To make the white background, copy template A on the facing page at 400 percent and trace it with a soft pencil onto tracing paper. Place the tracing paper face down and centered on the white sheet of card stock. Retrace the drawing to transfer it to the card stock.

5 Cut out the drawing along the outermost outline, and score and fold all the solid lines. Keep all lines toward the outside of the box shape. **(B)**

6 Add glue to the 4 smallest tabs and attach them to the rectangles that are perpendicular to each. Let the glue dry completely. The 2 longest tabs, which are attached to the edges of 2 sides, correspond to the top and bottom of the box.

Use stenciling to personalize the key holder—perhaps with a monogram or with a favorite design.

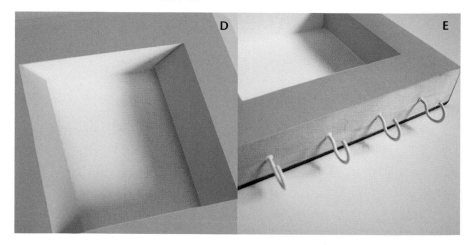

D E

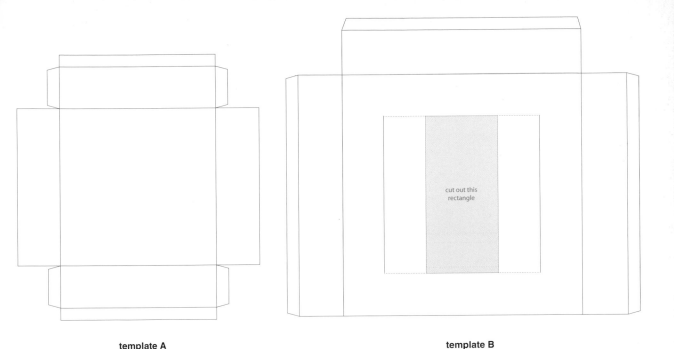

template A

template B

7 Center and glue the white box onto the cardboard background, resting the box above the wooden block. Make sure that the bottom tab folds flat onto the front side of the wooden block. Glue the underside of this tab to the wooden block.

8 To make the blue frame, copy template B, above, at 400 percent. Then trace the template with a pencil on tracing paper and transfer the tracing onto the blue card stock, following the same technique as in step 4. Cut out the center piece where indicated, and cut the slits at the top and bottom of each of the 2 small rectangles in the center. Score and fold all the other straight edges, leaving all the pencil marks on the inside of the frame. **(C)**

9 Center the blue frame over the white box (the side of the frame with no tabs should be at the bottom, over the wooden block). Glue the 3 outermost tabs (top center and right and left sides) around the back of the sheet of cardboard. Push the 2 center rectangles into the white box and glue them to the right and left sides of the box. **(D), (E)**

tip*

- Think about how many hooks you'll need
- before you start this project. With more
- hooks, there will be less space separating
- each, and you may need to adjust the
- measurements called for in step 3. You'll
- want to be sure the hooks are spread out
- evenly so that the keys will balance.

hooked-up key holder *127*

Flower Favor Box

This box would brighten up a range of events, such as a wedding, a baby shower, or a birthday celebration. A table with a display of several boxes can make any celebration more festive—just imagine everyone's reaction to these special handmade favors. This is a simple project to assemble, and the boxes can be easily enlarged if needed.

MATERIALS

1 sheet of tracing paper, 8½" x 11" (21.5cm x 28cm)

Pencil

1 sheet of green heavy-weight paper, 8½" x 11" (21.5cm x 28cm), such as card stock

Scissors

Bone folder

Glue stick

1 sheet of white heavy-weight paper, at least 2" (5cm) square, such as card stock

Compass

1 sheet of white lightweight paper, 20" (51cm) square, such as tissue paper

White PVA glue

FINISHED SIZE

2" x 3¾" x 2" (5cm x 9.5cm x 5cm)

TIME: 1–2 HOURS

(to make 4 boxes)

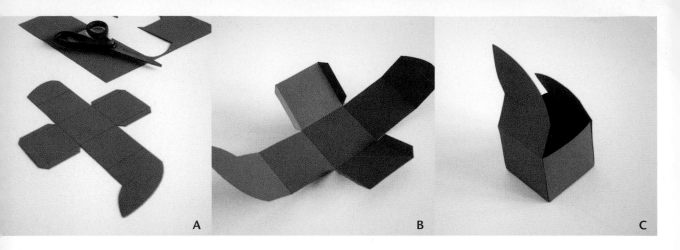

A   B   C

1 Copy the template on the facing page at 200 percent, and trace it onto tracing paper with a soft pencil. Place the tracing paper face down on the green card stock and retrace the drawing.

2 Cut out the drawing along the outer outline. Score and fold along the solid lines, keeping the pencil markings toward the inside of the box. Cut the slits, indicated by dotted lines, on each side of the template (adjacent to the sections that will make up the leaf). **(A), (B)**

3 Add glue using the glue stick to the outer side of the 4 small flaps, and press them against the inner sides of the squares that are perpendicular to each one. **(C)**

4 Once the glue is dry, close the box by sliding the 2 slits on each of the leaf areas into each other. The leaf will not be completely flat. **(D)**

5 To make the flower, draw and cut a circle that is 1½" (3.8cm) in diameter from the white card stock. **(E)**

6 Cut out 8 circles that are 2" (5cm) in diameter from the white tissue paper. Fold each circle in half twice (in other words, fold them into quarters), and keep them closed.

7 Add a pea-sized amount of PVA glue to the center of the white card stock circle. Distribute 4 folded circle wedges flat around the card stock with their points meeting in the center; the lines between the wedges will form a + shape.

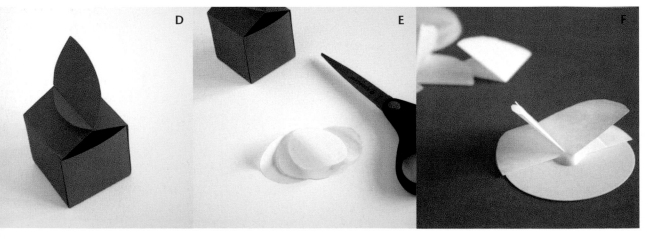

D   E   F

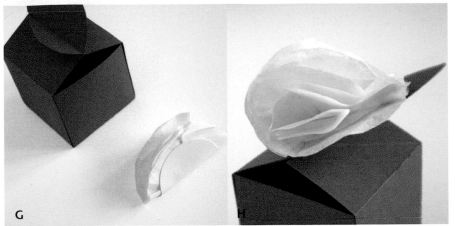

G

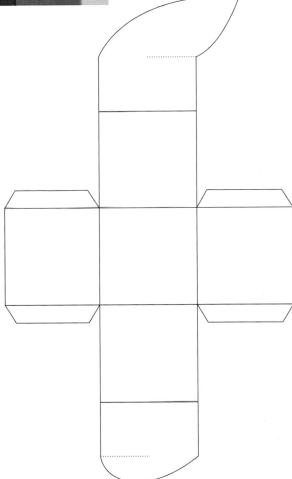

H

If needed, use the leaf of the box to write the guests' names. Labeled boxes can be used on a table setting instead of place card holders.

8 If needed, add a bit more glue to the center of the card stock circle (and above the 4 tissue paper wedges). Add the remaining 4 folded circle wedges in the same way as described in step 7, aligning each wedge directly on top of the 1 below. **(F)**

9 When the flower is completely dry, crease and fold it in half, then open it up again. Partially open each of the circles, being careful not to unglue them. As you open each of the petals, arrange them by lifting and slightly twisting the paper. When you're done, the flower will look similar to a carnation. **(G)**

10 Lay the flower on the box by matching the fold of the circle with the center and deepest part of the leaf. Attach the flower to the box by adding glue only to the side of the box that has the largest area of the leaf. Do not glue the other half of the flower to the opposite leaf area or the box won't open. **(H)**

tip*

- *Coordinate the favor box to the event by using colored*
- *tissue paper for the flowers. You can even alternate the*
- *colors of the circles that make up the flowers.*

Ribbon Handle Gift Box

This box was inspired by a small cylindrical purse I found in a toy store a couple of years ago. The placement of the ribbon handle is what really got my attention—it's the centerpiece of the design. I had never seen anything like it and just had to investigate its construction and make my own. This reinterpretation turns a simple box into something quite unique.

MATERIALS

2 sheets of tracing paper, 11" x 17" (28cm x 43cm)

Pencil

1 sheet of white heavy-weight paper, 12" (30.5cm) square, such as card stock

1 sheet of yellow heavy-weight paper, 12" (30.5cm) square, such as card stock

Scissors

Craft knife

Bone folder

1 orange ribbon, 1½" x 16" (3.8cm x 40.5cm)

White PVA glue

Glue stick

FINISHED SIZE

4¼" x 4¼" x 4 (11cm x 11cm x 10cm)

TIME: 1–2 HOURS . . . .

WATER FOR CHOCOLATE ■ LAURA ESQUIVEL

TO EACH HIS HOME

Bilyana Dimitrova

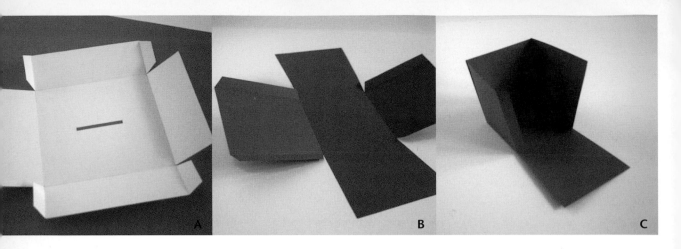

A

B

C

1 Copy the templates on the facing page at 250 percent, and trace them onto tracing paper with a soft pencil. Place the tracing of template B face down on the white card stock, and retrace. Place the tracing of template A face down on the yellow card stock and retrace.

2 Cut both drawings out of the card stock by following the outermost outline. Using a craft knife, cut the slit out of the center of the cover. Score and fold all the other solid lines, making sure to keep all pencil markings inside the box. Set the white cutout aside. **(A), (B)**

3 Using a glue stick, apply glue to the outer side of the four tabs of the yellow cutout. Fold and press each glued tab to the inside of the adjacent rectangle. Set aside to dry. **(C)**

4 Measure and cut a 3½" (9cm) square out the remaining white card stock paper. Measure and cut a ⅛" x 1⅝" (3mm x 4cm) slit that is centered on the square.

5 Fold the orange ribbon in half crosswise. Slide the folded end through the slit in the square made in step 3 until only 1" (2.5cm) of the 2 loose ends remains on the other side. Open up the ends, and attach each 1 to the square, on opposite sides of the slit, with PVA glue. Make sure the ribbon is completely secured to the card stock. **(D)**

tip*

A smaller version of this box can make a very cute favor box. Just copy the templates to the desired size. I use the templates at 165 percent to make favor boxes that are about 2½" (6.5cm) high.

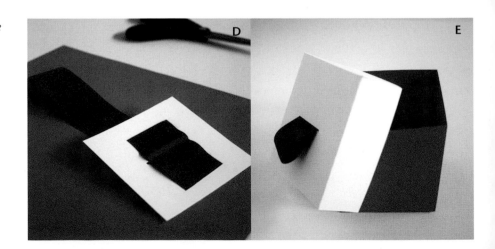

D

E

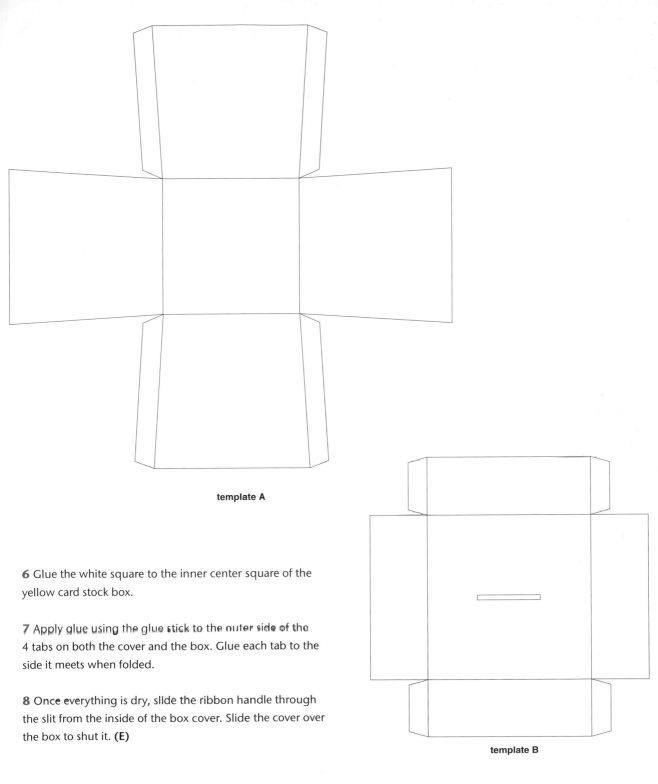

template A

template B

6 Glue the white square to the inner center square of the yellow card stock box.

7 Apply glue using the glue stick to the outer side of the 4 tabs on both the cover and the box. Glue each tab to the side it meets when folded.

8 Once everything is dry, slide the ribbon handle through the slit from the inside of the box cover. Slide the cover over the box to shut it. **(E)**

Pod Pattern Keepsake Box

Sometimes you just need more than an online photo album. A keepsake box can be a unique gift for a newly married couple in need of a special place for storing photos, cards, messages, and honeymoon souvenirs. It will become a creative way for your friends to remember their special day, and you can use their wedding colors for embellishment. This box would also be an excellent gift for other special occasions, such as a school graduation or a child's return from summer camp.

MATERIALS

1 sheet of white heavy-weight paper, 20" x 30" (51cm x 76cm), such as bristol paper

Ruler

Pencil

Scissors

White PVA glue

1 sheet of black heavy-weight paper, 12" (30.5cm) square, such as card stock

1 sheet of tracing paper, 8½" x 11" (21.5cm x 28cm)

Round hole punch, ¼" (6mm) diameter

1 sheet of the black-and-white section of the phone book

Glue stick

Ribbon, 13" x ⅜" (33cm x 9mm)

FINISHED SIZE

9¼" x 4¼" x 6" (23.5cm x 11cm x 15cm)

TIME: 2–3 HOURS. . . . .

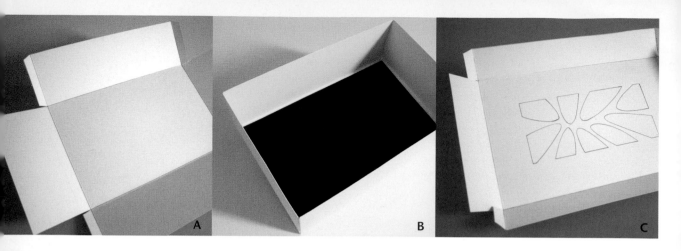

A B C

1 To make the base of the box, measure and cut a 15" x 12" (38cm x 30.5cm) rectangle of white bristol paper.

2 Draw a 9" x 3" (23cm x 7.5cm) rectangle centered on the long side of the rectangle.

3 Draw two ½" x 3" (13mm x 7.5cm) rectangles adjacent to and to the right and left of the rectangle drawn in step 2. (These will form tabs in step 7.)

4 Draw another rectangle that is below and adjacent to the rectangle made in step 2 and measures 9" x 6" (23cm x 15cm). This will be the bottom of the box.

5 Turn the whole sheet 180 degrees, and repeat steps 2 and 3.

6 Draw two 3" x 6" (7.5cm x 15cm) rectangles adjacent and to the right and left of the rectangle drawn in step 4. These rectangles will become the shorter sides of the box.

7 Cut the ½" (13mm) horizontal slits that attach each of the rectangles from step 3 to the rectangles made in step 6. Cut the outer corners of these rectangles on a diagonal. (Papercraft Secret, page 43).

8 Cut around the outline of the box. Score and fold all the straight edges of the rectangles, keeping the pencil markings toward the inside. (A)

9 Apply glue to the tabs drawn in step 3, and press them to the inside of the rectangles from step 6.

10 Measure and cut a 8¾" x 5¾" (22cm x 14.5cm) rectangle out of the black card stock. Center and glue the rectangle to the inside bottom of the box. (B)

11 To make the cover of the box, measure and cut a 12¼" x 9¼" (31cm x 23.5cm) rectangle of white paper.

12 Draw a 9¼" x 1½" (23.5cm x 3.8cm) rectangle centered on the edge of the long side of the white paper.

13 Draw two ½" x 1½" (13mm x 3.8cm) rectangles adjacent to and to the right and left of the rectangle drawn in step 12.

14 Draw another rectangle that is below and adjacent to the rectangle made in step 12 and measures 9¼" x 6¼" (23.5cm x 16cm). This will be the top of the box.

tip*

This box makes a great place to store mementos

from a vacation. In step 23, attach small cutouts of

photographs from the vacation to fit into the ovals on

the top cover instead of using the graphic phonebook

strips. You can also use appropriate paper—such as a

map—to line the insides of the top and the bottom of

the box.

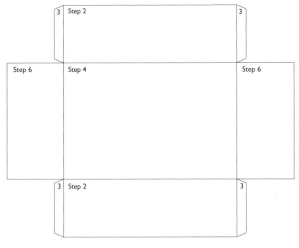

base of box

15 Turn the whole sheet 180 degrees and repeat steps 12 and 13.

16 Draw two 1½" x 6¼" (3.8cm x 16cm) rectangles adjacent to and to the right and left of the rectangle drawn in step 14. These rectangles will become the smaller ends of the cover.

17 Cut the ½" (13mm) horizontal slits that attach each of the rectangles from step 13 to the rectangle made in step 16. Then cut the slits that separate the 3 rectangles drawn in step 15. Cut the outer corners of these rectangles on a diagonal.

18 Cut around the entire outline of the box. Score and fold all the straight edges of the rectangles, keeping the pencil markings toward the inside.

19 Copy the template on page 141 and trace with a soft pencil. Place the tracing paper centered and face down on the rectangle made in step 14 and retrace the drawing. Cut out the negative spaces with a craft knife. **(C)**

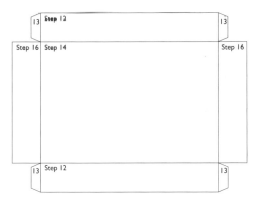

box cover

D

20 Punch out 2 holes that are ½" (13mm) apart from each other in the center of one of 1 rectangles made in step 12. Thread the ribbon through the holes and make a bow on the outside of the box.

21 Apply glue to the outer side of the rectangle tabs created in step 13, and press them to the inside of the rectangles from step 16. **(D)**

22 Measure and cut another 8¾" x 5¾" (22cm x 14.5cm) rectangle out of the black card stock.

23 Measure a 6½" x 3½" (16.5cm x 9cm) area of the phone book page and cut it into ⅛" (3mm) wide strips. Use the glue stick to attach the strips in parallel rows to the center of the black rectangle, leaving a very thin space in between each strips. **(E)**

24 Apply glue to the perimeter of the black sheet to attach it to the center inside of the top of the box. The strips of the phone book should appear through the cutout shapes.

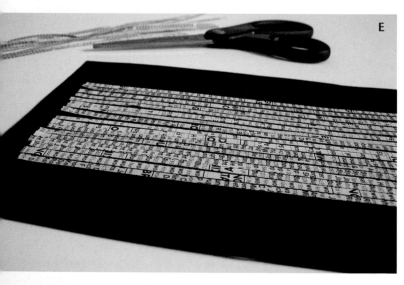

E

RESOURCES

The materials used for this book can be found in your local craft and office supply stores. The following online sources can be useful if you can't find something locally.

A. C. Moore
Tel: 866.342.8802
www.acmoore.com

Blick Art Materials
Tel: 800.933.2542
www.dickblick.com

Crafts Etc.
Tel: 800.888.0321
www.craftsetc.com

Creative Papers
Tel: 800.727.3740
www.handmade-paper.us

Jo-Ann
Tel: 888.739.4120
www.joann.com

Michaels
Tel: 800.MICHAELS
www.michaels.com

Oriental Trading
Tel: 800.875.8480
www.orientaltrading.com

Office Depot
Tel: 800.GO.DEPOT
www.officedepot.com

Office Max
Tel: 800.283.7674
www.officemax.com

Paper.com
Tel: 888.PAPER.GREAT
www.paper.com

Paper Source
Tel: 888.PAPER.11
www.paper-source.com

Papyrus
Tel: 800.789.1649
www.papyrusonline.com

Pearl
Tel: 800.451.PEARL
www.pearlpaint.com

Staples
Tel: 800.378.2753
www.staples.com

Texas Art Supply
Tel: 800.888.9278
www.texasart.com

ACKNOWLEDGMENTS

I never imagined that once I started down the path of working on handmade projects more frequently that I'd end up where I am today. A big reason why I've been more driven to explore new ideas is the inspiration that I have received from the craft bloggers that I've come to admire. They are also the reason why I started my own blog and jumped into the fray. I would have never started the adventure of writing this book had it not been for the renewed enthusiasm that I now feel for my work. My career path has been permanently changed, and I'm so appreciative of it all.

Thank you to the very talented team of people at Potter Craft: Melissa Bonventre, Rebecca Behan, Jennifer Graham, and Chi Ling Moy. Your efforts have made this book so much better than I ever could have imagined. My thanks also go to Kate McKean, my wonderful agent, who started this whole thing. Her guidance has been so invaluable. And to Sanford Schulwolf, whose photography I love looking at over and over again. And thanks to Kevin Kosbab, who went the extra mile with all his hard work.

Of course, special acknowledgments must extend to my family and friends, especially my loving husband Gustavo and my sweet children Daniel and Catalina. I must thank them for always being so supportive and truly interested in what I do. There is no way I would have made it without their endless amounts of encouragement and patience.